Guide to Accreditation

by the
National Academy
of Early Childhood
Programs

1987

Guide to Accreditation

by the
National Academy of
Early Childhood Programs

A Division of the
National Association for the
Education of Young Children

Sue Bredekamp, Editor

National Association for the Education of Young Children
1834 Connecticut Avenue, N.W., Washington, DC 20009-5786

Photo credits:
  Cleo Freelance Photo, p. vii, 1
  Vivienne della Grotta, p. vii, 197
  Betty C. Ford, p. vii, 5
  Bob Herbert, p. vii, 217
  Robert Meier, p. vii, 213
  Katherine Nell, p. vii, 15
  Rick Reinhard, p. vii, 101
  L.S. Stepanowicz, p. vii, 79
  Subjects & Predicates, p. vii, 113
  Elaine M. Ward, p. vii, 43

Copies of *Guide to Accreditation by the National Academy of Early Childhood Programs* are available from NAEYC, 1834 Connecticut Avenue, N.W., Washington, DC 20009-5786.

Second printing, November 1985. Third printing, December 1987. Fourth printing, April 1989. Fifth printing, March 1990.

Library of Congress Catalog Card Number: 85-60990
ISBN Catalog Number: 0-912674-93-8
NAEYC #16

Printed in the United States of America.

Pronoun references in this book are used only for editorial simplicity and are not intended to reflect stereotyped concepts of children or adults.

Contents

Foreword

The accreditation system of the National Academy of Early Childhood Programs represents more than three years of suggestions, recommendations, and hard work on the part of thousands of early childhood professionals throughout the United States. From the inception of the accreditation system, it has been based on the concept of collaboration. The development of the Academy's Criteria for High Quality Early Childhood Programs reflects the collaboration of early childhood program administrators, teachers, parents, researchers, teacher educators, and policy makers from all 50 states and several foreign countries.

This collaborative effort is further reflected in the accreditation process itself. The most important element in the accreditation system is the early childhood program's self-study which is an opportunity for everyone in the program—the administrators, teachers, teacher assistants, parents, and even the children—to work together to evaluate and improve the program. The next step is the on-site visit which is conducted by a validator—an early childhood professional whose role is to verify the program personnel's report of their own compliance with the Criteria. The validation process is part of this system because NAEYC and the Academy believe that for real and lasting program improvement to result, it must be initiated from within the program, not by outside evaluators. The final step in the process, the accreditation decision, is another collaborative effort. The accreditation decision is not based on achieving a certain number of points. Accreditation decisions are made by three-member Commissions who work as teams drawing on their diverse geographic, programmatic, and experiential backgrounds in applying professional judgment to the decision-making process.

The goal of the accreditation system is to improve the quality of care and education provided for young children in group programs. All children who participate in group programs deserve to benefit from the experience. All children in group programs must not only be safe and protected but must have the opportunity to experience an environment that enhances children's development. Achieving high quality programs for all children cannot be accomplished by inspecting centers, approving some and failing others. This goal of achieving high quality programs can be met only by providing programs with an incentive to improve and by providing resources and referrals to facilitate this improvement. For the accreditation project to achieve its goals, the entire early childhood community must work in the spirit of collaboration on which the system is founded.

What does accreditation mean for the field of early childhood education? Accreditation assists families in making decisions about their children's care and education. Accreditation offers agencies, employers, and other program supporters a system for identifying high quality programs. Accreditation provides program directors and teachers with guidelines for professional practice.

The initiation of a national, voluntary accreditation system for early childhood programs is a major step toward the professionalization of the field of early childhood education. The standards for accreditation were developed by the early childhood profession. They represent the current consensus on what defines a high quality program for young children. The accreditation system is the early childhood profession's definition of its standards for high quality programs and its recognition of those programs that provide high quality care and education for young children.

Just as the growth of a child is a gradual, developmental process, the implementation of a new concept or system needs fostering and time. The accreditation system of the National Academy of Early Childhood Programs is dynamic and will grow and develop during the system's early years of operation. Just as families take great pride in the developmental strides of young children, the self-esteem and public perception of the early childhood profession is enhanced by the existence of the Academy's accreditation system for high quality early childhood programs.

Marilyn M. Smith
Executive Director
NAEYC

Definitions

Academy—the National Academy of Early Childhood Programs, the division of the National Association for the Education of Young Children (NAEYC) that administers the accreditation system.

Administrator—person most responsible for the on-site, ongoing, daily supervision of the program and staff. The terms *administrator* and *director* are used interchangeably throughout these materials.

Centers—part-day and full-day group programs in schools and other facilities serving a minimum of ten children from the age of birth through five years and/or five- through eight-year-olds before and/or after school. See definition of *program*.

Chief administrative officer—person legally responsible for the business operation of the program. This person may or may not be the same person who directs the daily implementation of the program including the supervision of staff and curriculum.

Commissioners—early childhood professionals who meet in teams of three to make accreditation decisions.

Component—aspects of an early childhood program that are evaluated. The Criteria address ten components of an early childhood program: Interactions among Staff and Children; Curriculum; Staff-Parent Interaction; Staff Qualifications and Development; Administration; Staffing; Physical Environment; Health and Safety; Nutrition and Food Service; and Evaluation.

Criteria—standards by which the components of an early childhood program are judged. The complete list of the Academy's Criteria for High Quality Early Childhood Programs with Interpretations appears in the green book, *Accreditation Criteria and Procedures of the National Academy of Early Childhood Programs*.

Criterion—singular form of *Criteria*.

Director—see definition of *Administrator.*

Early Childhood—birth through eight years of age.

Early Childhood Classroom Observation—observation form used by teachers and directors to determine how well each group or classroom meets the criteria that are assessed through observation.

Group—children assigned to a staff member or team of staff members, occupying an individual classroom or well-defined physical space within a larger room.

Indicators—important points to look for in rating the quality of an early childhood classroom using the Academy's *Early Childhood Classroom Observation.*

Infants—children between the ages of birth and 12 months.

Parent—legal custodian of the child in the program.

Preschoolers—children from three through five years of age. Children in kindergarten are considered preschoolers in these materials.

Program—an early childhood program. The terms *center* and *program* are used interchangeably throughout these materials.

Program Description—form programs use to report their compliance with the Academy's Criteria to become accredited.

School-agers—children attending first grade or beyond who are participating in a before- and/or after-school program.

Staff—paid adults who have direct responsibilities for the care and education of the children.

Toddlers—children between the ages of 13 months and 36 months.

Validator—early childhood professional who conducts the on-site validation visit to verify the accuracy of the Program Description.

Section 1
Introduction to *Guide to Accreditation*

Introduction to *Guide to Accreditation*

The purpose of the National Academy of Early Childhood Programs is to improve the quality of care and education provided for young children in group programs in the United States. The Academy accomplishes this purpose by developing training resources, by providing public information about the importance of high quality early childhood programs, and by accrediting those programs that voluntarily demonstrate substantial compliance with the Academy's Criteria for High Quality Early Childhood Programs.

The accreditation process involves three steps:

Step 1—Program personnel conduct a self-study to determine how well the program meets the Academy's Criteria, make needed improvements, and report the compliance with the Criteria on the Program Description.

Step 2—Validators make an on-site visit to verify the accuracy of the Program Description.

Step 3—A three-person Commission considers the validated Program Description and makes the accreditation decision.

This book is designed to help program personnel through these steps. In this book you will find instructions and materials for conducting an in-depth self-study of an early childhood program, including sample copies of the Early Childhood Classroom Observation, Administrator Report, Staff Questionnaire, and Parent Questionnaire that are used during the self-study and in reporting your results. Multiple copies of these materials are provided to programs along with this book.

This book also includes a copy of the Program Description that is used by programs to report their compliance with the Criteria to the Academy. A description of the validation process and the accreditation decision is presented also.

This book is meant to be used with the green book, *Accreditation Criteria and Procedures of the National Academy of Early Childhood Programs*. In the green book you will find the complete list of the Academy's Criteria for High Quality Early Childhood Programs with interpretations. The Criteria are the basis for the entire accreditation system. If at any time a criterion needs clarification, please use the green book as a reference. Criteria are always referred to by the same letter and number.

The Criteria address all components of a high quality early childhood program—Interactions among Staff and Children, Curriculum, Staff-Parent Interaction, Staff Qualifications and Development, Administration, Staffing, Physical Environment, Health and Safety, Nutrition and Food Service, and Evaluation. The self-study process involves all the people who are part of an early childhood program—the administrators, staff, and parents. The children themselves are not overlooked as participants in the self-study. The primary purpose of the self-study is to examine the quality of life experienced by children in the program. Therefore, children are observed, and if old enough should be consulted, so that you gain an accurate understanding of what it is like to be a child in the program.

Early childhood personnel who choose to work toward accreditation for their programs demonstrate a professional commitment to self-evaluation and self-improvement. Programs accredited by the National Academy of Early Childhood Programs achieve professional and public recognition as providers of high quality care and education for young children.

Section 2
How to Do the Self-Study

How to Do the Self-Study

What is the self-study?

The self-study is a comprehensive and internal evaluation of all aspects of the early childhood program.

How is the self-study used?

The self-study is used by center personnel to systematically evaluate their program and identify areas in need of improvement. After improvements are made, the results are reported to the National Academy of Early Childhood Programs for use in making accreditation decisions.

What are the benefits of the self-study?

Taking an honest look at the program as it operates today is the first step toward making the improvements you need. One way to take an honest look is through the self-study. The self-study helps center staff and administrators analyze the strengths and weaknesses of the program, focus attention on areas in need of improvement, and also congratulate themselves for achieving and maintaining those areas that are clearly strengths.

The self-study can have many benefits. The self-study process can be a unifying force for a staff. A "we're-all-in-this-together" feeling can result as long as the self-study process is applied to the roles and responsibilities of all staff members—including the director! Emphasizing the common goal of improving the quality of the program can create a feeling of professionalism among the staff that is very stimulating. Also, any improvements in operating procedures, although the changes take time and effort, undoubtedly will result in greater cost effectiveness and improved service for children and families.

There are two ways to look at the self-study. It is similar to making a videotape of all the things that happen in your center. It can be threatening. It can also be an exciting and revealing experience. Because it is a *self*-study, *you* are making the videotape and *you* are deciding who will see it. Focusing on the potential for staff development, personal and professional growth, and an improved program for children and families will help the director and staff view self-study as an opportunity.

How should the self-study be conducted?

The self-study will be done by a variety of programs serving different populations and having different funding sources. As a result, the way in which the self-study is conducted will vary. Some centers have a large staff and many children, while others may serve fewer than 20 children with a very small staff. This *Guide* describes the few steps required of all centers participating in the process. Centers can be as creative as possible in adding other dimensions. There is no one right way to do the self-study. However, there is a *wrong* way.

What is the wrong *way to conduct the self-study?* The director acts alone, telling staff what they must do.

Staff members simply check off that they meet the criteria without thoughtful consideration and critical self-examination.

Staff members receive only criticism for what they are doing wrong without acknowledgment for what they are doing well.

Parents are not consulted.

Children are not observed closely to learn what really happens.

The self-study is rushed without adequate time given to reflect on and make necessary improvements.

The process is threatening; staff become defensive; children sense the stress.

Now that you know the *wrong* way to do the self-study, try to think of all the ways to make the self-study a positive, growth-enhancing experience for staff, parents, and children.

Who does the self-study?

The self-study is designed to involve all participants in an early childhood program—the administrators, teachers, assistants, parents, and even the children themselves. The word *self* refers to each person's involvement in examining her or his own contribution to the program.

What resources will be needed to conduct the self-study?

The *Guide* is designed to be comprehensive. Multiple copies of the Observation form and questionnaires are sent with the *Guide*. Academy staff can be contacted on a toll-free telephone number for assistance.

How long will it take?

The self-study is designed to be self-directed. The time needed will vary but ordinarily the self-study is expected to take from two to four months. The length of time is determined by the center and the improvements the staff wish to make. Regardless of how much time the center takes to get ready, the information that is sent to the Academy in the Program Description must be current and should reflect the existing situation, not what it was when the self-study began nor what the staff plans to do in the future.

What are the steps in the self-study?

These steps need to take place during the self-study.

Step 1—Introduce the concept to staff and parents. The self-study process is initiated and controlled by the center director. Admittedly, the self-study involves a significant commitment of time and effort by the director. But it cannot be a solitary effort. For the self-study to be successful, it must involve all the people who are likely to be affected—the staff members and parents—as soon as possible. The initial presentation of the concept to the staff is particularly important. Whenever evaluation is implied, people can be threatened. Therefore, it is important for the director to let staff know immediately that they are doing a fine job. Having their center accredited will help them get recognition for the high quality program they provide. Of course, the self-study will also identify aspects of the program that they may wish to change or improve, but they will be active participants in the evaluation process. Two videotapes may be ordered from NAEYC to help directors orient staff and parents—*Doing a Self-Study: Why and How* and *Using the Early Childhood Classroom Observation*.

Step 2—Collect information about the program from various sources including at least
    (a) Observations of each classroom or specific group in the center. Each classroom should be observed and rated using the *Early Childhood Classroom Observation* by at least the lead teacher and the director (or other appropriate person such as the program coordinator or a board member).
    (b) Evaluation of the administrative criteria by the director using the *Administrator Report* as a guide.
    (c) Evaluation of the program by the staff using the *Staff Questionnaire* as a guide.
    (d) Evaluation of the program by parents using the *Parent Questionnaire* as a guide.

Specific suggestions and directions for completing each of these parts of the self-study are presented in each section of the *Guide*.

Step 3—Plan for improvement and make changes where needed. If the self-study process is thorough, it will uncover both strengths and weaknesses of the program. Administrators and staff will identify aspects of the program where change is needed. It is likely that two different kinds of changes may be needed: (1) physical or technical changes, such as developing new procedures or rearranging classrooms, and (2) social or behavioral changes, such as implementing a more developmentally appropriate curriculum or developing better communication with parents, more cooperative staff relations, or more positive and supportive relations with children. In some situations, both kinds of changes are involved. For instance, clearly written program policies will facilitate parent communication to some extent, but they cannot replace personal contact.

Because it is often easier to make physical or technical changes, those changes could be made first. For example, it is relatively easy to rearrange materials and furniture or to write clear personnel policies. If the technical changes can be implemented successfully, a positive foundation for improvement will be established. Then the potentially more difficult social or curricular changes can be undertaken.

Making improvements in your program can be a challenging process. Here are some pointers to help you overcome the most common obstacles to change in early childhood programs:

■ Recognize that change is stressful.

Change can be a source of stress for people even when the change is a desirable one. But change is most stressful when the people involved do not control the change or do not participate in it. To minimize the stress, be sure to acknowledge the difficulties. Work together with the staff to establish priorities, suggest alternatives, try solutions, and agree on systems that work best in your program. Remember that for change to be real and lasting, the people who are most affected by the change must participate in it.

■ Recognize which change requires resources, and use limited resources wisely and carefully.

Too often, early childhood program personnel say that they could provide a much better program if only they had more money. It is true that some change is financially impossible. For example, equipping a playground or expanding indoor space may be prohibitively expensive. However, many aspects of the program can be improved without additional expense. For instance, it does not cost more money to speak kindly to children and to treat them with respect than it does to be harsh and punitive. However, to bring about such change in staff behavior, some additional staff training may be needed, for which funds may be limited. Do not overlook the many effective, low-cost training strategies now available. Contact the Academy or the Information Service at NAEYC for inexpensive training resources related to the Criteria or for referral to resources available in your area.

■ Change the things you can.

There will be aspects of the program that are easy to improve and some aspects that are difficult to change. For example, keeping better records of staff training is relatively easy to do and does not cost money, but correcting a problem playground may involve additional funding that is not available. The important thing to remember is that the accreditation process does not require 100% compliance with all the Criteria. Also, you will have the opportunity to indicate how you meet the Criteria a different way. For instance, you may develop alternative plans to provide a good outdoor play experience for children. Many of the Criteria can be met in different ways.

■ Decide whether to seek accreditation.

Once you have made the improvements you wish to make and feel that you meet the Criteria as best you can, then you need to decide whether to go on and seek accreditation for the program. You are not committed to doing so and may decide that the self-study was sufficient to meet your personal goals for program evaluation and improvement. But don't try to be perfect; accreditation is awarded for substantial compliance with the Criteria. If you decide to seek accreditation, your next step is to use the information you learned during the self-study to complete the Program Description.

Step 4—Prepare Program Description for use in validation and accreditation decision process. After improvements are made, the results are reported to the Academy on the Program Description form. A sample copy of the Program Description appears in Section 7 of the *Guide*. A clean copy to complete and return to the Academy is sent with the *Guide*.

The Program Description form is designed to ensure uniformity in reporting and to facilitate use by validators and commissioners making accreditation decisions. The Program Description has three parts. Part 1 is the Center Profile that provides general information about how the program is staffed and organized. Part 2 presents the center's compliance with the criteria that are observed using the Classroom Observation. Part 3 presents the center's compliance with the administrative criteria that are assessed by the director. Some of these criteria are also assessed by the staff and/or parents on the questionnaires.

Specific directions for completing the Program Description appear in Section 7 of the *Guide*.

Where do we begin?

This *Guide* is designed to help you through the self-study and validation. As with anything new, it may seem complicated at first, but it will become clearer with experience. Familiarize yourself with the tasks before presenting the concepts to staff members. Break down each task into parts and establish dates to serve as goals for completing each step. The chart on pages 12 to 14 will help.

Remember that although the Academy requires certain steps in the self-study, you should not be limited by those requirements. Depending on the unique features of your program, you may want to introduce other elements such as participation by board members who may be asked to evaluate the program using the Administrator Report. The potential benefits of the self-study/accreditation process will be achieved only if each program individualizes the process to its own needs and strengths. Be as creative as you like in examining your program; and if something works particularly well, share your ideas with the Academy so that other directors may benefit.

Always keep sight of your goal—to provide the best quality program for young children and their families.

Task and Timeline Chart

The purpose of this chart is to help program directors develop their own individualized plan for completing all the self-study tasks. Fill in the names of the people responsible for each task, and also identify dates to serve as goals for completing each task.

TASK	PERSON(S) RESPONSIBLE	GOAL DATES

Orientation

1. Review the *Guide* and instructions.

Director (or person responsible for coordinating the self-study).

2. Meet with staff to go over project and give instructions.

Director

Self-study and program improvement

3. Observe and rate each classroom using Classroom Observation form.

Staff observe and rate their own classrooms.

4. Observe and rate each classroom using Observation form.

Director (or other appropriate person) observes and rates each classroom.

5. Meet with individual staff to discuss results and plan for improvement.

Director (or other appropriate person)

6. Evaluate program using Administrator Report as your workbook. Collect information on Staffing and Staff Qualifications to summarize on Center Profile.

Director

TASK	PERSON(S) RESPONSIBLE	GOAL DATES
7. Staff evaluate program using Staff Questionnaire as a guide. (Use staff meetings, interviews, Staff Survey for discussion.)	Director (or staff member assigned this task)	_____
8. Evaluate criteria related to parents using Parent Questionnaire as a guide. (Use parent meetings, interviews, Parent Survey for discussion.)	Director (or parent or staff member assigned this task)	_____
9. Other tasks you wish to add to study and improve your program:		
_____	_____	_____
_____	_____	_____
_____	_____	_____
_____	_____	_____
_____	_____	_____
_____	_____	_____

Program Description

If you choose to seek accreditation, the remaining tasks are part of collecting the current information that goes into the Program Description.

TASK	PERSON(S) RESPONSIBLE	GOAL DATES
10. Meet with individual staff to decide on agreed-upon ratings on Observation form to be reported to Academy on Classroom Observation Summary Sheet. (These ratings will take place after improvements have been made.)	Director	_____
11. Tabulate results of Classroom Observation Summary Sheet, and compute average ratings.	Director	_____

TASK	PERSON(S) RESPONSIBLE	GOAL DATES
12. Distribute Staff Questionnaire to staff.	Director	_____
13. Complete Staff Questionnaire.	Each staff member who works directly with children.	_____
14. Summarize results of Staff Questionnaire on Summary Sheet.	Director or staff member assigned to this task.	_____
15. Distribute Parent Questionnaire to parents. (Request return within three days or ask that the questionnaire be completed at the center.)	Staff members	_____
16. Remind parents to return questionnaire. (Post notice or send home reminder.)	Staff members	_____
17. Summarize results of Parent Questionnaire on Summary Sheet.	Director or parent or staff member assigned this task.	_____
18. Compile Program Description using Administrator Report and Center Profile and summary sheets of (1) Classroom Observations (2) Staff Questionnaire (3) Parent Questionnaire	Director	_____
19. Mail Program Description, Classroom Observation Summary Sheet, and check for validation fee to the Academy in envelope provided. Do *not* send Parent and Staff Questionnaires or their Summary Sheets but keep those for the validation visit.	Director	_____

Mail your Program Description in time to allow the Academy at least 30 working days to arrange your validation visit.

Early Childhood Classroom Observation

Directions for use

Sample Observation Form

Sample Summary Sheet

Early Childhood Classroom Observation

Directions for use

What is the purpose of the Early Childhood Classroom Observation?

Many of the Academy's Criteria for High Quality Early Childhood Programs relate to what happens to children in classrooms. To determine how well a program meets those criteria, observations of individual classrooms (or groups) must be done. The Early Childhood Classroom Observation includes only the criteria from the complete list that are to be observed in each classroom. The Observation form is a three-point rating scale. The letters and numbers of the items on the Observation form refer to the complete list of Criteria in the green book. Sometimes the exact wording of the item differs because the language has been changed to make the item more observable.

Who uses the Early Childhood Classroom Observation?

Each lead teacher for each individual classroom (or clearly defined group of children) uses the form to observe and rate the quality of her or his own classroom. The director (or other appropriate person) observes and rates each classroom independently. A sample copy of the Early Childhood Classroom Observation is in this section of the *Guide*. Multiple copies of the Observation form (on buff paper) are sent with the *Guide*. Specific directions appear on the Observation form.

When is the Observation done?

Teachers should take some time to become familiar with the form before they begin to observe and rate their classroom. Because teachers cannot observe their own behavior, they will have to think about what they usually do before they can assign a rating to some items. The Observation takes about one and one-half hours to complete.

The director (or other appropriate administrator) also observes and rates each classroom. Teachers may want to make improvements in their classrooms before they are observed by the director. The director's observation should be done during the peak period of activity while the children are present (usually the morning hours). The director may not see evidence for a specific item during the observation period of one to two hours in each classroom. If so, the director should ask the teacher open-ended questions to obtain information about those items (for example, "What happens when children arrive?") or should return to the classroom at different times. In full-day programs, the director should return to the classroom in the afternoon to observe how the quality of interactions is maintained throughout the day.

How are the results used?

Teachers and the director should independently observe and rate the classroom. Then, they should compare their ratings, identify strengths and weaknesses, and develop a plan for making needed improvements.

The process of comparing ratings can be a positive, developmental experience or it can be threatening for teachers, depending on how it is handled. To make this process as constructive as possible, try these suggestions. Write down the teacher's and director's ratings for each item. There will probably be more agreements than disagreements. Begin by pointing out how many times you both agreed and by commenting on the aspects of the classroom that rated most highly. Where differences arise in ratings, the director begins by explaining why she rated the item as she did. For instance, "I gave it a 2 because during the time I observed I saw you interacting very positively with children, but all your attention was taken up with Jamie and Anton." This type of communication, where the director describes what she saw from her own point of view is easier for the teacher to accept than a more accusing message that might make the teacher feel defensive. For example, compare the earlier statement with this one that is based on the same observation—"You obviously prefer Jamie and Anton to the other children because you spend all your time talking to Jamie and Anton while ignoring the rest of the group."

Sometimes ratings of teachers and directors will not be the same because a criterion is interpreted differently. When there is a disagreement about a rating, one way of resolving the problem is to refer to the green book which has the complete statement of the criterion and its interpretation, or refer to NAEYC's *Developmentally Appropriate Practice.*

Once teachers feel that they have made the improvements they wish to make, the director and teacher agree on a rating for each item to report for that classroom.

How are the results reported on the Program Description?

Observations provide a great deal of information about each classroom. However, the accreditation applies to the entire program, not the individual teachers. Therefore, the results of observations are averaged across classrooms and the average score is reported as the center's rating for the criteria that are observed. For example, out of three classrooms in a center, two may have excellent materials rating a 3, and one may lack some variety, rating a 2. The score for the center on the materials criterion would be a 2.7. (3 + 3 + 2 = 8. 8 ÷ 3 = 2.7.)

A summary sheet for the observations is provided to help the director tabulate the center's average ratings. These ratings are reported on Part 2 of the Program Description (Section 7). A sample Summary Sheet appears on p. 41 of the *Guide.* A clean copy of the Classroom Observation Summary Sheet with space for reporting results of 12 classrooms is sent with the *Guide.*

How is the summary sheet filled out?

Copy the ratings for each classroom. These ratings will be the ratings agreed upon by the teacher and director after improvements are made. They must be a whole number, either a 3, 2, or 1. Total the ratings across all classrooms and record the sum total for each criterion. Divide the sum total by the number of observations to get the average rating across classrooms for each criterion. (Space is also provided to calculate an average total score for each classroom. However, this information is not needed by the Academy and is included for your use only.)

Program Code

Early Childhood Classroom Observation

SAMPLE

Group or classroom being observed _____

Number of children in group _____   Number of volunteers _____

Number of paid staff present _____

Age range of children in group—youngest to oldest (in years/months) _____

Person observing   ☐ Teacher   ☐ Director   ☐ Validator

Observation date _____ and Time _____

Instructions

What is the purpose of this form?

This form is to help you observe and rate the level of quality of your early childhood program. Each item is related to the Academy's Criteria for High Quality Early Childhood Programs. The letters and numbers to the left of each item refer to a specific criterion that is found in *Accreditation Criteria and Procedures of the National Academy of Early Childhood Programs* (green book).

Who uses this form?

Each separate group in a center must be observed by the lead teacher and the director who are to complete their forms independently. The teacher and director should discuss their ratings after each completes the form. Then the teacher and director agree on a rating to report to the Academy after improvements are made. The validator also uses this form to observe during the validation visit.

How do I use this form?

Each boldface statement on the left side of the page is the criterion to be rated. Many criteria are followed by a list of indicators that *must* be considered in the rating. Indicators (important points to look for) are listed next to a box ☐. Put a check mark in the box as you observe the indicator. Examples are sometimes provided to help define the Criteria. These specific examples do not have to be observed, but something similar should be seen. Rate each criterion using the following scale:

[1] Not met	[2] Partially met	[3] Fully met
The criterion is not met.	The criterion is partially met.	The criterion is completely met.
You observe **little evidence** that this statement accurately describes the program.	You observe **some evidence** that this statement accurately describes the program.	You observe **a great deal of evidence** that this statement accurately describes the program *throughout the day*.
The behavior happens **rarely or seldom.**	The behavior happens **some of the time.**	In order for a criterion to rate a [3], all indicators (☐) related to the age group being observed *must be* present. (It is possible for all indicators to be present without rating the criterion a [3].)
		The behavior happens **most of the time.**

Rate the criterion by circling only **one** of the numbers [1] or [2] or [3].
Explain your ratings under the "Comments" column if
 ■ the criterion is not met [1]
 ■ the criterion is partially met [2]
 ■ the criterion could be met another way (List the way and explain why.)

What if I do not see evidence for an item during the observation time?

Your ratings should be based on what happens typically in the program.

 ■ *A teacher* who does not see evidence for an item during the observation should rate the item based on what happens typically. Please do not rate the item based on what you would like to have happen or plan to try in the future.

 ■ *A director or visiting observer* who does not see evidence for an item during the observation should interview the lead teacher following the observation and ask open-ended questions to obtain information about the item. An open-ended question does not suggest possible answers. For example, "What happens when the children arrive?" or "What do you do when children hit each other?" are open-ended questions. It is important that directors do not base their ratings on the policy of the program or what they believe ought to happen in the classroom. When a rating is based on what a teacher says rather than what is observed, write an "R" for report on the Observation form.

 In some cases, criteria (or indicators or examples) relate to specific age groups, such as infants, or specific kinds of programs. If you are not observing that age group or if the criterion does not apply to the program, please check the box marked "not applicable."

Suggestions for using this form

1. Read over the entire Observation form before beginning to rate a classroom.

2. The director or outside observer should spend 10 to 15 minutes becoming familiar with the classroom before beginning to assign ratings.

3. The items on the form do not need to be completed in order. Some criteria are rated more easily than others and these can be done first. Start with the criteria observed most easily such as items for Physical Environment **(G)** and Health and Safety **(H).**

4. If children move among more than one teacher (between learning centers, for example), follow the children and base your rating on the quality of the children's overall experience.

5. When more than one teacher is observed with a group, base the ratings on all adults in the group who interact with the children. Rule of thumb: rate criteria on the quality of the children's experience.

6. If there are no clearly defined groups in separate spaces, follow what is happening to a sample of an age group of children.

7. Do not feel pressured to rate a criterion too quickly. If you relax, observe, and gain a sense of what is happening, it is easier to make a rating decision.

Definitions

In early childhood programs, children are grouped in a variety of ways—by chronological age, developmental age, or multi-age grouping. These definitions are to simplify the use of this form, not to recommend a way of grouping children.

Group: The children assigned to a staff member or team of staff members, occupying an individual classroom or well-defined physical space within a larger room.

Staff: Adults who have direct responsibility for the care and education of the children.

Infants: Children between the ages of birth and 12 months.

Toddlers: Children between the ages of 13 months and 36 months.

Younger toddlers: Children from the age of 13 months to between 18 and 24 months.

Older toddlers: Children between the ages of 24 and 30 months to 36 months.

Preschoolers: Children from the age of three years through five years. Children in kindergarten are considered preschoolers in these materials.

School-agers: Children attending first grade or beyond who are participating in a before- and/or after-school program.

A. Interactions among Staff and Children

CRITERION	Not met	Partially met	Fully met	COMMENTS

RATING

A-1. Staff interact frequently with children showing affection and respect.
- ☐ Staff interact nonverbally by smiling, touching, holding.
- ☐ Staff talk with individual children during routines (arriving/departing, eating) and activities.

Rating: 1 2 3

A-2. Staff are responsive to children.
- ☐ Quickly comfort infants in distress.
- ☐ Reassure crying toddlers.
- ☐ Listen to children with attention and respect.
- ☐ Respond to children's questions and requests.

Rating: 1 2 3

A-3a. Staff speak with children in a friendly, courteous manner.
- ☐ Speak with individual children often.
- ☐ Speak with children at their eye level.
- ☐ Call children by name.

Rating: 1 2 3

A-3b. Staff talk with individual children, and encourage children of all ages to use language.

For example:

Repeat infants' sounds, talk about things toddlers see, help two-year-olds name things, ask preschoolers open-ended questions, provide opportunities for school-agers to talk about their day.

Rating: 1 2 3

A-4a. Staff treat children of all races, religions, and cultures equally with respect and consideration.

Rating: 1 2 3

A. Interactions among Staff and Children *continued*

CRITERION	RATING			COMMENTS
	Not met	Partially met	Fully met	

A-4b. Staff provide children of both sexes with equal opportunities to take part in all activities.

| 1 | 2 | 3 |

A-5. Staff encourage independence in children as they are ready.

| 1 | 2 | 3 |

For example:

Infants: finger feeding self.

Toddlers: washing hands, selecting own toys.

Threes and fours: dressing, picking up toys.

Fives: setting table, cleaning, acquiring self-help skills.

School-agers: performing responsible jobs, participating in community activities.

A-6a. Staff use positive approaches to help children behave constructively.

| 1 | 2 | 3 |

Guidance methods include

☐ Redirection.

☐ Planning ahead to prevent problems.

☐ Positive reinforcement and encouragement.

☐ Consistent, clear rules explained to children.

A-6b. Staff do *not* use physical punishment or other negative discipline methods that hurt, frighten, or humiliate children.

| 1 | 2 | 3 |

A-7. Overall sound of group is pleasant most of the time.

| 1 | 2 | 3 |

For example:

Happy laughter, excitement, busy activity, relaxed talking.

Adult voices that do not dominate.

A. Interactions among Staff and Children *continued*

CRITERION	RATING			COMMENTS
	Not met	Partially met	Fully met	

A-8a. **Children are generally comfortable, relaxed, and happy, and involved in play and other activities.** [1] [2] [3]

A-8b. **Staff help children deal with anger, sadness, and frustration.** [1] [2] [3]

A-9. **Staff encourage prosocial behaviors in children such as cooperating, helping, taking turns, talking to solve problems.** [1] [2] [3]

☐ Adults model the desired behaviors.

☐ Adults praise prosocial behaviors.

A-10. **Staff expectations of children's social behavior are developmentally appropriate.** [1] [2] [3]

For example:

Two pieces of the same equipment are available so toddlers are not forced to share too often.

Preschoolers are encouraged to cooperate in small groups.

School-agers have opportunities to participate in group games or to work or play alone.

A-11. **Children are encouraged to talk about feelings and ideas instead of solving problems with force.** [1] [2] [3]

For example:

Adults supply appropriate words for infants and toddlers to help them learn ways to get along in a group.

Adults discuss alternative solutions with children two years and older.

B. Curriculum

(Note: A page is not missing. The letters and numbers are not in consecutive order because only some of the Criteria are observed in each classroom.)

CRITERION	RATING			COMMENTS
	Not met	Partially met	Fully met	
	1	2	3	

B-3a. Modifications are made in the environment, schedule, and activities to meet child's special needs.

☐ Not applicable

For example:

Indoor and outdoor environments are accessible to special needs child including ramps, bathroom, and playground access as needed.

Schedule is modified as needed, such as shorter day or alternative activities.

Program is modified as needed, such as provision of special materials and equipment, use of supportive services, individualization of activity.

B-4. The daily schedule provides a balance of activities on the following dimensions:

B-4a. Indoor/outdoor   1   2   3

B-4b. Quiet/active   1   2   3

B-4c. Individual/small group/large group   1   2   3

B-4d. Large muscle/small muscle   1   2   3

B-4e. Child initiated/staff initiated   1   2   3

B. Curriculum *continued*

CRITERION	RATING			COMMENTS
	Not met	Partially met	Fully met	

B-5a. Multiracial, nonsexist, nonstereotyping pictures, dolls, books, and materials are available.

RATING: [1] [2] [3]

B-5b. Developmentally appropriate materials and equipment are available for *infants*.

RATING: [1] [2] [3]

☐ Not applicable

☐ Rattles, squeak toys, music.
☐ Cuddly toys.
☐ Teething toys.
☐ Mobiles, unbreakable mirrors, bright objects and pictures.
☐ Infant seats, crawling area, sturdy furniture to pull up self.

B-5c. Developmentally appropriate materials and equipment are available for *toddlers*.

RATING: [1] [2] [3]

☐ Not applicable

☐ Push and pull toys.
☐ Stacking toys, large wooden spools/beads/cubes.
☐ Sturdy picture books, music.
☐ Pounding bench, simple puzzles.
☐ Play telephone, dolls, pretend toys.
☐ Large paper, crayons.
☐ Sturdy furniture to hold on to while walking.
☐ Sand and water toys.

B. Curriculum *continued*

CRITERION	RATING			COMMENTS
	Not met	Partially met	Fully met	
	1	**2**	**3**	

B-5d. Developmentally appropriate materials and equipment are available for *preschoolers*.

☐ Active play equipment for climbing and balancing.

☐ Unit blocks and accessories.

☐ Puzzles, manipulative toys.

☐ Picture books and records, musical instruments.

☐ Art materials such as finger and tempera paints, crayons, scissors, paste.

☐ Dramatic play materials such as dolls, dress-up clothes and props, child-sized furniture, puppets.

☐ Sand and water toys.

☐ Not applicable

B-5e. Developmentally appropriate materials and equipment are available for *school-agers*.

1	**2**	**3**

☐ Not applicable

☐ Active play equipment and materials such as bats and balls for organized games.

☐ Construction materials for woodworking, blocks.

☐ Materials for hobby and art projects, science projects.

☐ Materials for dramatics, cooking.

☐ Books, records, musical instruments.

☐ Board and card games.

B. Curriculum *continued*

CRITERION

B-7. **Staff provide a variety of developmentally appropriate hands-on activities for children to achieve the following goals:**
(Rate each goal separately considering the examples related to the age group being observed.)

	RATING			COMMENTS
	Not met	Partially met	Fully met	
	1	2	3	

B-7a. **Foster positive self-concept.**

For example:

Infants/younger toddlers

Hold, pat, and touch babies for comfort and stimulation.

Talk and sing to babies.

Imitate each baby's actions and sounds.

Play mirror games, label facial features and body parts.

Allow infants to feed themselves when ready.

Encourage and support each baby's developmental achievements such as pulling up self.

Older toddlers/preschoolers

Allow time for children to talk about what they see, do, and like.

Use children's names frequently in songs, games.

Display children's work and photos of children.

Encourage children to draw pictures, tell stories about self and family.

School-agers

Provide opportunities to express growing independence/self-reliance such as the ability to make choices, initiate own activities.

Allow opportunities to work or play alone.

B-7b. **Develop social skills.**

1	2	3

For example:

Infants/younger toddlers

Hold, pat, and touch babies.

Talk to, sing to, and play with each baby on a one-to-one basis.

Respond to and expand on cues coming from child.

Interpret infants' actions to other children to help them get along in the group ("Mary had it first.").

Older toddlers/preschoolers

Assist toddlers in social interaction.

Create space and time for small groups of children to build blocks together or enjoy dramatic play.

Provide opportunities for sharing, caring, and helping, such as making cards for a sick child or caring for pets.

School-agers

Arrange planned and spontaneous activities in team sports, group games, interest clubs, board and card games.

Allow time to sit and talk with friend or adult.

B. Curriculum *continued*

CRITERION	RATING			COMMENTS
	Not met	Partially met	Fully met	

B-7c. Encourage children to think, reason, question, and experiment.

[1]   [2]   [3]

For example:

Infants/younger toddlers

Provide a stimulating, safe environment for infants and toddlers to explore and manipulate.

Provide pictures, mobiles, brightly colored objects for babies to look at, reach for, and grasp.

Play naming and hiding games such as peek-a-boo, pat-a-cake.

Provide rattles, squeak toys, other noise-making objects for babies to hear.

Move or carry around noncrawling infants so they can see different things and people.

Older toddlers/preschoolers

Plan activities for labeling, classifying, sorting objects by shape, color, size.

Discuss daily and weekly routines in terms of time concepts, season of the year.

Observe natural events such as seeds growing, life cycle of pets.

Create opportunities to use numbers, counting objects.

Take walks around building or neighborhood.

Plan trips to provide new learning experiences for preschoolers.

Encourage water and sand play.

School-agers

Provide activities such as cooking, money-making projects, gardening, science experiments, trips in the community, interacting with visitors, multicultural experiences, computer projects.

B-7d. Encourage language development.

[1]   [2]   [3]

For example:

Infants/younger toddlers

Look at simple books and pictures. Talk to, sing to, and play with babies throughout the day.

Label objects and events.

Use action rhymes.

Encourage imitation by repeating child's gestures and attempts at words.

Play verbal games, have informal conversations.

Respond to sounds infant makes.

Older toddlers/preschoolers

Read books, tell stories about experiences, talk about pictures.

Provide time for conversation, ask child questions that require more than a one-word answer.

Answer children's questions.

Add more information to what child says.

Label things in room, use written words with pictures and spoken language.

Use flannel board, puppets, songs, finger plays.

School-agers

Provide opportunities to read books.

Write and produce plays, publish newspapers, write stories.

Share experiences with friends or adults.

Use audio-visual equipment such as tape recorders.

Make own filmstrips.

B. Curriculum *continued*

CRITERION	RATING			COMMENTS
	Not met	Partially met	Fully met	

B-7e. Enhance physical development.

1	2	3

For example:

Infants/younger toddlers
Provide open carpeted space for crawling.
Provide low sturdy furniture for child to pull up self or hold on to while walking.
Provide outdoor activities for infants.
Provide objects for infants to reach for and grasp.
Allow mobile infants to move about freely, play with and explore the environment.

Older toddlers/preschoolers
Provide time and space for active play such as jumping, running, balancing, climbing, riding tricycles.
Provide creative movement activity using obstacle course or activity songs and records.
Provide fine-motor activities such as stacking rings, popbeads, pegboards, and puzzles for toddlers; add lacing cards and woodworking for preschoolers.

School-agers
Provide opportunities to get physical exercise, use variety of outdoor equipment.
Encourage participation in group games, individual and team sports.
Provide fine-motor activities and hobbies such as sewing, macramé, pottery, leatherwork, carpentry.

B-7f. Encourage and demonstrate sound health, safety, and nutritional practices.

1	2	3

For example:

All ages
Cook and serve a variety of nutritious foods.
Discuss good nutrition.
Do activities to develop safety awareness in the center, home, and community.
Encourage health practices such as washing hands, brushing teeth, getting regular exercise and enough rest.
Talk about visiting doctor, dentist.

B-7g. Encourage creative expression and appreciation for the arts.

1	2	3

For example:

Infants/younger toddlers
Encourage scribbling with crayons.
Use music, records.
Sing to baby.

Older toddlers/preschoolers
Do creative art activities such as brush painting, finger painting, drawing, collage, and playdough.
Provide time and space for dancing, movement activities, creative dramatics.
Do musical activities such as singing, listening to records, playing instruments.

School-agers
Provide planned and spontaneous activities in arts and crafts such as mural and easel painting, ceramics, carpentry, weaving.
Encourage dancing, creative dramatics, record playing, singing, playing instruments.

B. Curriculum *continued*

CRITERION			RATING		COMMENTS
	Not met	Partially met	Fully met		

B-7h. Respect cultural diversity.

For example:

All ages

Cook and serve foods from various cultures.

Celebrate holidays of various cultures.

Read books, show pictures of various cultures.

Invite parents and other visitors to share arts, crafts, music, dress, and stories of various cultures.

Take trips to museums, cultural resources of community.

Rating: 1 (Not met) · 2 (Partially met) · 3 (Fully met)

B-8. Staff provide materials and time for children to select their own activities during the day.

☐ Infants and toddlers have some materials for free choice.

☐ Several alternative activities are available for preschooler's choice.

☐ Staff respect the child's right not to participate in some activities.

☐ Teachers pick up on activities that children start, or interests that children show.

☐ School-agers help prepare materials, plan and choose their own activities most of the time.

Rating: 1 · 2 · 3

B-9. Staff conduct smooth and unregimented transitions between activities.

☐ Children are told to get ready for transition ahead of time.

☐ Children are not always required to move as a group from one activity to another.

☐ The new activity is prepared before the transition from the completed activity to avoid waiting.

☐ School-age children help plan and participate in the change of activity, have time to adjust to change from school to center.

Rating: 1 · 2 · 3

B. Curriculum *continued*

CRITERION	RATING			COMMENTS
	Not met	Partially met	Fully met	

B-10. Staff are flexible enough to change planned or routine activities.

	Not met 1	Partially met 2	Fully met 3

For example:

Staff follow needs or interests of the children.

Staff adjust to changes in weather or other unexpected situations in a relaxed way without upsetting children.

B-11. Routine tasks such as diapering, toileting, eating, dressing, and sleeping are handled in a relaxed and individual manner.

	1	2	3

☐ Routine tasks are used as opportunities for pleasant conversation and playful interaction to bring about children's learning.

☐ Self-help skills are encouraged as children are ready.

☐ Routines are tailored to children's needs and rhythms as much as possible.

For example:

Respecting infants' individual sleeping schedules, providing alternatives for preschoolers who are early risers, providing school-agers with a place to rest if they choose, respecting school-agers' increasing interest in personal grooming.

G. Physical Environment

G-1a. There is enough usable space indoors so children are not crowded.

	1	2	3

G. Physical Environment *continued*

CRITERION	RATING			COMMENTS
	Not met	Partially met	Fully met	

G-1b. There is enough usable space for outdoor play for each age group.

☐ 1   ☐ 2   ☐ 3

For example:

Age groups use different areas or are scheduled at different times.

G-2. Space is arranged to accommodate children individually, in small groups, and in a large group.

☐ 1   ☐ 2   ☐ 3

☐ There are clear pathways for children to move from one area to another without disturbing activities.

☐ Areas are organized for easy supervision by staff.

G-3. Space is arranged to facilitate a variety of activities for each age group.

☐ 1   ☐ 2   ☐ 3

☐ Nonwalkers are provided open space for crawling and protected space for play.

☐ Toddlers and preschoolers have space arranged for a variety of individual and small group activities including block building, dramatic play, art, music, science, math, manipulatives, quiet book reading.

☐ Sand and water play and woodworking are available on regular occasions.

☐ School-agers are provided separate space for their program including both active and quiet activities.

G. Physical Environment *continued*

CRITERION	RATING			COMMENTS
	Not met	Partially met	Fully met	

G-4. A variety of age-appropriate materials and equipment are available for children indoors and outdoors.

| | 1 | 2 | 3 | |

☐ A sufficient quantity of materials and equipment is provided to avoid problems with sharing or waiting.

☐ Materials are durable and in good repair.

☐ Materials are organized consistently on low, open shelves to encourage independent use by children.

☐ Extra materials are accessible to staff to add variety to usual activities.

G-5. Individual space is provided for each child's belongings.

| | 1 | 2 | 3 | |

☐ There is a place to hang clothing.

☐ There are places for storing extra clothing and other belongings such as art work to be taken home.

G-6. Private areas where children can play or work alone or with a friend are available indoors and outdoors.

| | 1 | 2 | 3 | |

For example:

Book corners, lofts, tunnels, or playhouses that are easy for adults to supervise.

G-7. The environment includes soft elements.

| | 1 | 2 | 3 | |

For example:

Rugs, cushions, rocking chairs, soft furniture, soft toys, and adults who cuddle children in their laps.

G. Physical Environment *continued*

CRITERION	RATING			COMMENTS
	Not met	Partially met	Fully met	

G-8. Sound-absorbing materials such as ceiling tile and rugs are used to cut down noise.

[1] [2] [3]

G-9a. A variety of activities can go on outdoors throughout the year.

[1] [2] [3]

☐ Balance of shade and sun.

☐ Variety of surfaces such as hardtop for wheel toys, grass for rolling, sand and soil for digging.

☐ Variety of age-appropriate equipment for riding, climbing, balancing, individual playing.

G-9b. The outdoor play area is protected from access to streets and other dangers.

[1] [2] [3]

H. Health and Safety

H-7. Children are under adult supervision at all times.

[1] [2] [3]

For example:

Infants and toddlers are never left unattended.

Preschoolers are supervised by sight and sound.

School-agers may not be in sight, but staff know where children are and what they are doing.

H-12. Children are dressed appropriately for active play indoors and outdoors.

[1] [2] [3]

☐ Extra clothing is kept on hand.

☐ Protective clothing such as smocks and mittens is kept on hand.

H. Health and Safety *continued*

CRITERION	RATING			COMMENTS
	Not met	Partially met	Fully met	

H-13a. As children use the facility, staff and children keep areas reasonably clean.

☐ Tables are washed and floors are swept after meals.

☐ Toys are picked up after use.

1   2   3

H-13b. Toileting and diapering areas are sanitary.

☐ Soiled diapers are disposed of or held for laundry in closed containers out of reach of children.

☐ Cover of changing table is disinfected or disposed after each use.

☐ Toilet area is sanitized daily.

1   2   3

H-14a. Staff wash their hands with soap and water before feeding, preparing or serving food, and after diapering or assisting children with toileting or nose wiping.

1   2   3

H-14b. A sink with running hot and cold water is very close to diapering and toileting areas.

1   2   3

H-15a. The building, play yard, and all equipment are maintained in safe, clean condition and in good repair.

☐ No sharp edges, splinters, protruding or rusty nails, or missing parts.

1   2   3

H. Health and Safety *continued*

CRITERION	RATING	COMMENTS
	Not met / Partially met / Fully met	

H-15b. Infants' and toddlers' toys are large enough to prevent swallowing or choking.

| 1 | 2 | 3 |

☐ Not applicable

_____
_____
_____
_____
_____
_____

H-16b. Sides of infants' cribs are in a locked position when cribs are occupied.

| 1 | 2 | 3 |

☐ Not applicable

_____
_____
_____
_____
_____

H-17a. Toilets, drinking water, and handwashing facilities are easily accessible to children.

For example:

Facilities are either child sized or made accessible by nonslip stools.

| 1 | 2 | 3 |

_____
_____
_____
_____

H-17b. Soap and disposable towels are provided.

| 1 | 2 | 3 |

_____
_____
_____
_____
_____
_____

H-17c. Children wash hands after toileting and before meals.

| 1 | 2 | 3 |

_____
_____
_____
_____
_____
_____
_____

H-18a. Areas used by children are well-lighted and ventilated and kept at a comfortable temperature.

| 1 | 2 | 3 |

_____
_____
_____
_____
_____

H. Health and Safety *continued*

CRITERION	RATING			COMMENTS
	Not met	Partially met	Fully met	

H-18b. Electrical outlets are covered with protective caps. (NA for rooms used by school-agers only.)

[1] [2] [3]

☐ Not applicable

H-18c. Floor coverings are attached to the floor or backed with nonslip materials.

[1] [2] [3]

H-19a. Cushioning materials such as mats, wood chips, or sand are used under climbing equipment, slides, and swings.

[1] [2] [3]

H-19b. Climbing equipment, swings, and large pieces of furniture are securely anchored.

[1] [2] [3]

For example:

Permanent equipment outdoors, tall storage shelves indoors.

H-20. All chemicals and potentially dangerous products such as medicines or cleaning supplies are stored in original, labeled containers in locked cabinets inaccessible to children.

[1] [2] [3]

I. Nutrition and Food Service

CRITERION	RATING			COMMENTS
	Not met	Partially met	Fully met	
I-3. Mealtime is a pleasant social and learning experience for children.	1	2	3	

☐ Infants are held and talked to while bottle fed.

☐ At least one adult sits with children during meals to provide a good role model and encourage conversation.

☐ Toddlers and preschoolers are encouraged to serve and feed themselves.

☐ Chairs, tables, and eating utensils are suitable for the size and developmental levels of the children.

Program Code

Classroom Observation Summary Sheet

CRITERION REFERENCE NUMBER	ROOM 1	2	3	4	5	6	7	8	9	10	11	12	Sum of scores	Number of ratings	Average rating
GROUP NAME															
LEAD TEACHER															
A-1															
A-2															
A-3a															
A-3b															
A-4a															
A-4b															
A-5															
A-6a															
A-6b															
A-7															
A-8a															
A-8b															
A-9															
A-10															
A-11															
B-3a															
B-4a															
B-4b															
B-4c															
B-4d															
B-4e															
B-5a															
B-5b															
B-5c															
B-5d															
B-5e															
B-7a															
B-7b															
B-7c															
B-7d															
B-7e															
B-7f															
B-7g															
B-7h															

Classroom Observation Summary Sheet (continued)

CRITERION REFERENCE NUMBER	ROOM 1	2	3	4	5	6	7	8	9	10	11	12	Sum of scores	Number of ratings	Average rating
	RATING														
B-8															
B-9															
B-10															
B-11															
G-1a															
G-1b															
G-2															
G-3															
G-4															
G-5															
G-6															
G-7															
G-8															
G-9a															
G-9b															
H-7															
H-12															
H-13a															
H-13b															
H-14a															
H-14b															
H-15a															
H-15b															
H-16b															
H-17a															
H-17b															
H-17c															
H-18a															
H-18b															
H-18c															
H-19a															
H-19b															
H-20															
I-3															
Total score															
Number of items rated															
Average rating															

Section 4

Administrator Report and Center Profile

Directions for use

Sample Administrator Report

Sample Center Profile

List of Documents
Worksheet on Staff Qualifications

Administrator Report and Center Profile

Directions for use

What is the purpose of the Administrator Report and Center Profile?

Many of the Academy's Criteria for High Quality Early Childhood Programs address centerwide policies and procedures that are established for the entire program. This section includes

(a) an *Administrator Report* where the director rates the criteria that relate to the administration of the entire program. The Administrator Report uses the same three-point rating scale that is used on the Observation form and the Staff Questionnaire; and

(b) a *Center Profile* where the director reports factual information about the program such as staff qualifications, ages and numbers of children enrolled, and the number of staff to children. Some of this information is related to specific criteria, but for validators and commissioners to understand the program, it is necessary to report it in some detail.

The Administrator Report is used by the director (and other administrators if appropriate) as a workbook during the self-study to evaluate the program and identify needed improvements. The Center Profile is part of the Program Description that is completed if the program seeks accreditation. *If you do not wish to pursue accreditation, you do not need to complete the Center Profile.*

This section of the *Guide* also includes a List of Documents (pp. 75–76) that are required by the Criteria. If you wish to pursue accreditation, these documents should be collected in a central location or the location should be noted on pp. 75–76 to assist the validator during the visit.

Who completes the Administrator Report and Center Profile?

The Administrator Report and Center Profile are completed by the director or program administrator who is most responsible for the on-site, on-going daily supervision of the program. An owner who is not on-site on a daily basis would not be able to complete these reports.

How is the Administrator Report prepared?

The Administrator Report includes those criteria that are evaluated by the director for the entire program. A sample copy of the Administrator Report appears in this section of the *Guide*. A clean copy of the Administrator Report (on green paper) is sent with the *Guide*. Because one person completes this report, there is no need for a summary sheet.

How is the Center Profile prepared?

The Center Profile asks some specific questions about the hours of operation, funding sources, licensing, and other general information about the program that should be easily answered by the director. The Center Profile also includes two charts that summarize a great deal of information about the program. One chart reports the Staffing Pattern (Question 10) and the other chart reports Staff Qualifications (Question 11). Because these charts may seem a little complicated, samples are provided in this section of the *Guide* to show how the charts are to be completed.

The Staffing Pattern chart is designed to present information about enrollment, grouping, staff-child ratios, and the hours of staff members throughout the day. If your program operates longer than 6:00 a.m. to 7:00 p.m., you will need to adjust this chart.

The Staff Qualifications chart is used to describe the education and experience of the administrators and all staff who work directly with children. To help the director collect information about staff qualifications, a sample worksheet (p. 77) is provided in this section of the *Guide* that can be duplicated and distributed to staff members. Then the information from the worksheets can easily be transferred to the Staff Qualifications chart. Staff training in Early Childhood Education/Child Development is reported in units with one unit equal to 16 classroom hours or 1 semester hour of study. Staff should be sure to report all forms of training they have experienced, including workshops, conferences, and in-service training, not just formal courses.

How are the results reported on the Program Description?

Part 1 of the Program Description is the Center Profile. The director simply fills in the information on the Program Description. The criteria that are rated by the director on the Administrator Report are reported on Part 3 of the Program Description in the column marked "Director's rating and comments." The director should rate these criteria based on the situation after improvements have been made.

Administrator Report

Many of the Academy's Criteria for High Quality Early Childhood Programs require written documents or procedures that are established by the administrator for the entire program. This report includes the criteria that should be rated by the administrator. The letters and numbers next to each statement refer to the complete list of Criteria. This is why the letters and numbers may not be in consecutive order. (Refer to the green book, *Accreditation Criteria and Procedures,* for more detailed information on each criterion.)

Instructions

Evaluate the early childhood program that you administer by rating the degree to which each criterion in the report describes your program:

1 Not met	2 Partially met	3 Fully met
The criterion is not met.	The criterion is partially met.	The criterion is completely met.
There is **little evidence** that this statement accurately describes the program.	There is **some evidence** that this statement accurately describes the program.	There is **a great deal of evidence** that this statement accurately describes the program.

Rate each criterion by circling only **one** of the numbers: 1 or 2 or 3.

Explain your ratings under the "Comments" column in all of the following cases:

- the criterion is not met 1
- the criterion is partially met 2
- the criterion is met through an alternate means (Explain how and why.)

This report is for your use only during the self-study. If you decide to pursue accreditation, you will report how your center meets these criteria on Part 3 of the Program Description in the column marked, "Director's Rating."

48

B. Curriculum

CRITERION	RATING			COMMENTS
	Not met	Partially met	Fully met	

B-1. A long range, written curriculum plan that reflects the program's philosophy and goals for children is available.   □1 □2 □3

B-2. Staff plan realistic curriculum goals for children based on assessment of individual needs and interests.   □1 □2 □3

B-3a. Modifications are made in the environment when necessary for children with special needs.   □1 □2 □3
□ Not applicable

B-3b. Staff make appropriate professional referrals when necessary.   □1 □2 □3

B-4. For each group of children a written daily schedule is planned to achieve a balance of activities on the following dimensions:
a. Indoor/outdoor   □1 □2 □3
b. Quiet/active   □1 □2 □3
c. Individual/small group large group   □1 □2 □3
d. Large muscle/small muscle   □1 □2 □3
e. Child initiated/staff initiated   □1 □2 □3

C. Staff-Parent Interaction

CRITERION	RATING			COMMENTS
	Not met	Partially met	Fully met	
C-1a. A written description of the program's philosophy is available to parents.	1	2	3	
C-1b. Written operating policies are available to parents.	1	2	3	
C-2. A process exists for orienting children and parents to the center that may include a pre-enrollment visit, parent orientation meeting, or gradual introduction of children to the center.	1	2	3	
C-3. Staff and parents communicate about home and center childrearing practices in order to minimize potential conflicts and confusion for children.	1	2	3	
C-4a. Parents are welcome visitors in the center at all times (for example, to observe, eat lunch with a child, or volunteer to help in the classroom).	1	2	3	
C-4b. Parents and other family members are encouraged to be involved in the program in various ways.	1	2	3	

C. Staff-Parent Interaction *continued*

CRITERION	RATING			COMMENTS
	Not met	Partially met	Fully met	

C-5a. A verbal and/or written system is established for sharing day-to-day happenings that affect children. | 1 | 2 | 3 |

C-5b. Changes in a child's physical or emotional state are reported to parents regularly. | 1 | 2 | 3 |

C-6. Conferences are held at least once a year and at other times, as needed, to discuss children's progress, accomplishments, and difficulties at home and at the center. | 1 | 2 | 3 |

C-7. Parents are informed about the center's program through regular newsletters, bulletin boards, frequent notes, telephone calls, and other similar measures. | 1 | 2 | 3 |

D. Staff Qualifications and Development

(Refer to Staff Qualifications in Center Profile.)

D-1a. Staff who work directly with children are 18 years of age or older. | 1 | 2 | 3 |

D. Staff Qualifications and Development *continued*

CRITERION	RATING			COMMENTS
	Not met	Partially met	Fully met	

D-1b. Early Childhood Teacher Assistants (staff who implement program activities under direct supervision) are high school graduates or the equivalent and participate in professional development programs.

1	2	3

Out of _____
(total number of)
teacher assistants,

_____ meet these qualifications.

D-1c. Early Childhood Associate Teachers and Early Childhood Teachers (staff who are responsible for the care and education of a group of children) have at least a CDA Credential or an A.A. degree in Early Childhood/Child Development or equivalent.

1	2	3

Out of _____
(total number of)
teachers,

_____ meet these qualifications.

D-1d. Staff working with school-age children have training in child development, recreation, or a related field.

1	2	3

☐ Not applicable

D-1e. If staff members do not meet the specified qualifications, a training plan, both individualized and centerwide, has been developed and is being implemented for those staff members. Training is appropriate to the age group with which the staff member is working. *(Present training plan and evidence of ongoing, in-service training.)*

1	2	3

D-2a. The chief administrative officer (director or other appropriate administrator) of the center has training and/or experience in business administration.

1	2	3

D. Staff Qualifications and Development *continued*

CRITERION	RATING			COMMENTS
	Not met	Partially met	Fully met	

D-2b. An Early Childhood Specialist (an individual with a B.A. degree in Early Childhood Education/ Child Development and at least three years of full-time teaching experience with young children and/ or a graduate degree in ECE/CD) is employed to direct the educational program (may be the director or other appropriate person).

| 1 | 2 | 3 |

D-3. New staff are adequately oriented about the goals and philosophy of the center, emergency health and safety procedures, special needs of children assigned to the staff member's care, guidance and classroom management techniques, and planned daily activities of the center.

| 1 | 2 | 3 |

D-4a. The center provides regular training opportunities for staff to improve skills in working with children and families. Staff are expected to take part in regular training and professional development. The training may include workshops and seminars, visits to other programs, resource materials, in-service sessions, or course work.

| 1 | 2 | 3 |

D-4b. Training addresses the following areas: health and safety, child growth and development, planning learning activities, guidance and discipline techniques, linkages with community services, communication and relations with families, detecting and reporting child abuse and neglect, or other areas as needed.

| 1 | 2 | 3 |

D. Staff Qualifications and Development *continued*

CRITERION	RATING			COMMENTS
	Not met	Partially met	Fully met	

D-5. Accurate and current records are kept of staff qualifications including transcripts, certificates, or other documentation of continuing in-service education.

1	2	3

_____
_____
_____
_____
_____

E. Administration

E-1. At least annually, the director and staff conduct an assessment to identify strengths and weaknesses of the program and to set program goals for the year.

1	2	3

_____
_____
_____
_____
_____

E-2. The center has written policies and procedures for operating including hours, fees, illness, holidays, and refund information.

1	2	3

_____
_____
_____
_____
_____

E-3a. The center has written personnel policies including job descriptions, compensation, resignation and termination, benefits, and grievance procedures.

1	2	3

_____
_____
_____
_____
_____

E-3b. Hiring practices are nondiscriminatory. *(Present copy of advertised position or other evidence of equal opportunity employment.)*

1	2	3

_____
_____
_____
_____

E. Administration *continued*

CRITERION	RATING			COMMENTS
	Not met	Partially met	Fully met	
E-4. Benefits for full-time staff include at least medical insurance coverage, sick leave, annual leave, and Social Security or some other retirement plan.	1	2	3	
E-5a. Attendance records are kept.	1	2	3	
E-5b. Confidential personnel files are kept including résumés with record of experience, transcripts of education, documentation of in-service training, and results of performance evaluation. (See criterion **J-1.**)	1	2	3	
E-6a. In cases where the center is governed by a board of directors, the center has written policies defining roles and responsibilities of board members and staff.	1	2	3 ☐ Not applicable	
E-6b. Records of board meetings (minutes) are kept.	1	2	3 ☐ Not applicable	
E-7. Fiscal records are kept with evidence of long range budgeting and sound financial planning (projections of at least one year are needed).	1	2	3	

E. Administration *continued*

CRITERION	RATING			COMMENTS
	Not met	Partially met	Fully met	
E-8. Accident protection and liability insurance coverage is maintained for children and adults. *(Present policy and/or most recent canceled check or receipt for payment.)*	1	2	3	
E-9. The director (or other appropriate person) is familiar with and makes appropriate use of community resources including social services; mental and physical health agencies; and educational programs such as museums, libraries, and neighborhood centers.	1	2	3	
E-10a. Staff and administrators communicate frequently.	1	2	3	
E-10b. Staff plan and consult together.	1	2	3	
E-10c. Regular staff meetings are held for staff to consult on program planning, plan for individual children, and discuss working conditions (may be meetings of small group or full staff).	1	2	3	

E. Administration *continued*

CRITERION	RATING			COMMENTS
	Not met	Partially met	Fully met	

E-10d. Staff are provided paid planning time. [1] [2] [3]

E-11. Staff are provided space and time away from children during the day. (When staff work directly with children for more than four hours, staff are provided breaks of at least 15 minutes in each four hour period.) [1] [2] [3]

F. Staffing

(Refer to group size and staff-child ratio information in Center Profile)

F-1 and F-2. Staff-child ratios within group size

Age of children*	Group size									
	6	8	10	12	14	16	18	20	22	24
Infants (birth–12mos.)	1:3	1:4								
Toddlers (12–24 mos.)	1:3	1:4	1:5	1:4						
Two-year-olds (24–36 mos.)		1:4	1:5	1:6**						
Two- and three-year-olds			1:5	1:6	1:7**					
Three-year-olds					1:7	1:8	1:9	1:10**		
Four-year-olds						1:8	1:9	1:10**		
Four- and five-year-olds						1:8	1:9	1:10**		
Five-year-olds						1:8	1:9	1:10		
Six- to eight-year-olds (school age)								1:10	1:11	1:12

* Multi-age grouping is both permissible and desirable. When infants are not included, the staff-child ratio and group size requirements shall be based on the age of the majority of the children in the group. When infants are included, ratios and group size for infants must be maintained.

** Smaller group sizes and lower staff-child ratios are optimal. Larger group sizes and higher staff-child ratios are acceptable only in cases where staff are highly qualified (see Staff Qualifications, **D-1** and **D-2**).

F-1. The number of children in a group is limited to facilitate adult-child interaction and constructive activity among children. Groups of children may be age-determined or multi-age. *(Using the chart above, determine which groups meet or exceed the required group sizes.)* [1] [2] [3]

Out of _____ groups,
(total number of)
_____ groups meet group size requirements.

F. Staffing *continued*

CRITERION	RATING			COMMENTS
	Not met	Partially met	Fully met	

F-2a. Enough staff with primary responsibility for working with children are available to provide frequent personal contact, meaningful learning activities, and supervision, and to offer immediate care as needed.
(Using the chart above, determine which groups meet or exceed the required staff-child ratios.)

1	2	3

Out of _____ groups,
(total number of)
_____ groups meet staff-child ratio requirements.

F-2b. Substitutes are provided to maintain staff-child ratios when regular staff are absent.

1	2	3

F-3a. Each staff member has primary responsibility for and develops a deeper attachment to an identified group of children.

1	2	3

F-3b. Every attempt is made to have continuity of adults who work with children, particularly infants and toddlers.

1	2	3

F-3c. Infants and toddlers spend the majority of the time interacting with the same person each day.

1	2	3

☐ Not applicable

G. Physical Environment

CRITERION	RATING			COMMENTS
	Not met	Partially met	Fully met	

G-1a. There is a minimum of 35 square feet of usable playroom floor space per child indoors.

1	2	3

Please give actual square feet if less than 35 square feet _____.

G-1b. There is a minimum of 75 square feet of play space outdoors per child (when space is in use).

1	2	3

Please give actual square feet if less than 75 square feet

_____ .

H. Health and Safety

H-1. The center is licensed or accredited by the appropriate state/local agencies. If exempt from licensing, the center demonstrates compliance with its own state regulations for child care centers subject to licensing.

1	2	3

H-2a. Staff health records include results of pre-employment physical, results of tuberculosis test (within last two years), and emergency contact information.

1	2	3

H-2b. New staff members serve a probationary period of employment during which their physical and psychological competence for working with children is evaluated.

1	2	3

H. Health and Safety *continued*

CRITERION		RATING			COMMENTS
		Not met	Partially met	Fully met	

H-3. Child health records include results of recent health examination, up-to-date record of immunizations, emergency contact information, names of people authorized to call for the child, and important health history (such as allergies, chronic illness).

1	2	3

H-4. The center has a written policy specifying limitations on attendance of sick children. Provisions are made for the notification of the sick child's parents, the comfort of the child, and the protection of well children.

1	2	3

H-5. Provisions are made for safe arrival and departure of all children that also allow for parent-staff interaction. A system exists for ensuring that children are released only to authorized people.

1	2	3

H-6. If transportation is provided for children by the center, vehicles are equipped with age-appropriate restraint devices, and appropriate safety precautions are taken.

1	2	3

☐ Not applicable

H-8. Staff are alert to the health of each child. Individual medical problems and accidents are recorded and reported to staff and parents, and a written record is kept of such incidents.

1	2	3

H. Health and Safety *continued*

CRITERION	RATING			COMMENTS
	Not met	Partially met	Fully met	

H-9a. Staff know procedures for reporting suspected incidents of child abuse and/or neglect.

`1` `2` `3`

H-9b. Suspected incidents of child abuse and/or neglect by parents, staff, or other persons are reported to appropriate local agencies.

`1` `2` `3`

H-10. At least one staff member who has certification in emergency first-aid treatment and CPR is always in the center. Current certificates are kept on file.

`1` `2` `3`

H-11a. Adequate first-aid supplies are readily available.

`1` `2` `3`

H-11b. A plan exists for dealing with medical emergencies that includes a source of emergency care, written parental consent forms, and transportation arrangements.

`1` `2` `3`

H-13a. The facility is cleaned daily, including disinfecting bathroom fixtures and removing trash.

`1` `2` `3`

H. Health and Safety *continued*

CRITERION	RATING			COMMENTS
	Not met	Partially met	Fully met	

H-13b. Infants' equipment is washed and disinfected at least twice a week. Toys that are mouthed are washed daily.

☐ 1 ☐ 2 ☐ 3

☐ Not applicable

_____
_____
_____
_____

H-16a. Individual bedding is washed once a week and used by only one child between washings. Individual cribs, cots, or mats are washed if soiled.

☐ 1 ☐ 2 ☐ 3

☐ Not applicable

_____
_____
_____
_____

H-17. Hot water does not exceed 110° F (43° C) at outlets used by children.

☐ 1 ☐ 2 ☐ 3

_____
_____
_____
_____

H-18d. Nontoxic building materials are used.

☐ 1 ☐ 2 ☐ 3

_____
_____
_____
_____

H-18e. Stairways are well-lighted and equipped with handrails.

☐ 1 ☐ 2 ☐ 3

☐ Not applicable

_____
_____
_____
_____

H-18f. Screens are placed on all windows that open (when appropriate).

☐ 1 ☐ 2 ☐ 3

_____
_____
_____

H. Health and Safety *continued*

CRITERION	RATING			COMMENTS
	Not met	Partially met	Fully met	
H-20a. All chemicals and potentially dangerous products such as medicines or cleaning supplies are stored in original, labeled containers in locked cabinets inaccessible to children.	1	2	3	
H-20b. Medication is administered to children only when a written order is submitted by a parent, and the medication is administered by a consistently designated staff member. Written records are kept of medication given to children.	1	2	3	
H-21a. Staff are familiar with primary and secondary evacuation routes and practice evacuation procedures monthly with children.	1	2	3	
H-21b. Written emergency procedures are posted in conspicuous places.	1	2	3	
H-22a. Staff are familiar with emergency procedures such as operation of fire extinguishers and procedures for severe storm warnings (where necessary).	1	2	3	

H. Health and Safety *continued*

CRITERION	Not met	Partially met	Fully met	COMMENTS
		RATING		

H-22b. Smoke detectors and fire extinguishers are provided and periodically checked.

1   2   3

H-22c. Emergency telephone numbers including police, fire, rescue, and poison control services are posted by telephones.

1   2   3

I. Nutrition and Food Service

I-1. Meals and/or snacks are planned to meet the child's nutritional requirements in proportion to the amount of time the child is in the program each day, as recommended by the Child Care Food Program of the U.S. Department of Agriculture.

1   2   3

I-2a. Written menus are provided for parents.

1   2   3

I-2b. Feeding times and food consumption information is provided to parents of infants and toddlers at the end of each day.

1   2   3

☐ Not applicable

I. Nutrition and Food Service *continued*

CRITERION	RATING			COMMENTS
	Not met	Partially met	Fully met	

I-3. Foods indicative of children's cultural backgrounds are served periodically.

☐ 1 ☐ 2 ☐ 3

_____
_____
_____
_____

I-4. Food brought from home is stored appropriately until consumed.

☐ 1 ☐ 2 ☐ 3

☐ Not applicable

_____
_____
_____
_____

I-5. Where food is prepared on the premises, the center is in compliance with legal requirements for food preparation and service. Food may be prepared at an approved facility and transported to the program in appropriate sanitary containers and at appropriate temperatures.

☐ 1 ☐ 2 ☐ 3

_____
_____
_____
_____

J. Evaluation

J-1a. All staff are evaluated at least annually by the director or other appropriate supervisor.

☐ 1 ☐ 2 ☐ 3

_____
_____
_____
_____

J-1b. Results of staff evaluations are written and confidential. They are discussed privately with the staff member.

☐ 1 ☐ 2 ☐ 3

_____
_____
_____
_____

J. **Evaluation** *continued*

CRITERION	RATING Not met	Partially met	Fully met	COMMENTS
J-1c. Staff evaluations include classroom observation.	1	2	3	
J-1d. Staff are informed of evaluation criteria in advance.	1	2	3	
J-1e. Staff have an opportunity to evaluate their own performance.	1	2	3	
J-1f. A plan for staff training is generated from the evaluation process.	1	2	3	
J-2. At least once a year, staff, other professionals, and parents are involved in evaluating the program's effectiveness in meeting the needs of children and parents.	1	2	3	
J-3. Individual descriptions of children's development are written and compiled as a basis for planning appropriate learning activities, as a means of facilitating optimal development of each child, and as records for use in communications with parents.	1	2	3	

Program Code

Early Childhood Program Description
Part 1—Center Profile

Program identification—This page is removed before the Commission considers the Program Description.

Name of program **Everywhere Child Development Center**

Name and title of person completing this form **Jane Doe, Director**

Name and title of person legally responsible for administration of program (if different from above)

Jane and John Doe, owners

Location of program

Street **1234 Main St.**

City **Everywhere** State **MD** ZIP **20785**

Phone **(301) 555-1212**

To be completed during on-site visit

Validator(s) _____

Date of validation visit _____

Program Code

Early Childhood Program Description
Part 1—Center Profile

SAMPLE

1. How long has the program been operating at this site? _____ **5/6** _____
   (years/months)

2. Does the program currently meet local licensing regulations?

   If yes, by what agencies is the center licensed? **State Health Dept.**

   _____

   If no, explain _____

   _____

3. Describe the hours of operation of the program. **7:00 a.m. to 5:30 p.m.**

   Days per week **Monday to Friday**   Months per year **12**
   (specify months if less than 12)

4. What funding sources support the program?
   Provide estimated percentage of funding received from each source.

   100 % Parent tuition   _____ Church contributions

   _____ Public funds (federal/state)   _____ Employer contributions

   _____ Community funds (United Way, etc.)   _____ Other (please specify below)

   _____

   _____

5. If the program has a governing board or policy or advisory group, describe the composition of the group
   and its function.

   Group of nine parents function as advisory group.

6. What is the purpose of the program? (Describe the type of program, for example, a full-day child care center, half-day preschool, parent cooperative, Head Start, Montessori school, etc.)

Full-day child care center with half-day preschool and mother's day out program.

7. What is the philosophy of the program? (Provide a brief description of the program's goals and objectives for children. Use the space below or attach additional sheets if necessary.)

(Individual to each program.)

8. What is the total number of children enrolled in the center? _____65_____

   Daily enrollment (if different from total above) ___53___ Monday ___53___ Tuesday ___65___ Wednesday ___53___ Thursday ___53___ Friday ___—___ Saturday ___—___ Sunday

9. Provide the number of children enrolled by developmental level.

   ___0___ Infants (birth through 12 months)

   ___12___ Toddlers (13 months to 35 months)

   ___53___ Preschoolers (three- through five-year-olds)

   ___0___ School-agers (six-year-olds and older)

10. Staffing Pattern—use the following chart to describe how the program is staffed. For each hour of the day indicate the number of children enrolled in the group, the staff members assigned to the group (use initials or first names only), and the hours worked by the staff members. A *group* is the number of children assigned to a staff member or team of staff members occupying an individual classroom or well-defined space within a larger room.

Staffing Pattern

GROUP OF CHILDREN	STAFFING PATTERN													

Group name: Mother's Day Out Wednesday's only

AM	NUMBER OF CHILDREN ENROLLED EACH HOUR												PM
6:00	7:00	8:00	9:00	10:00	11:00	12:00	1:00	2:00	3:00	4:00	5:00	6:00	7:00
			12	12	12	12							

Number	Age	Hours of each staff member
	Infants	9:00 _____ Joan _____ 1:00
12	Toddlers (18 mos. to 30 mos.)	9:00 _____ Donna _____ 1:00
	Preschoolers	
	School-agers	

Group name: 3-yr. old group (30 mos. to 48 mos.)

AM	NUMBER OF CHILDREN ENROLLED EACH HOUR												PM
6:00	7:00	8:00	9:00	10:00	11:00	12:00	1:00	2:00	3:00	4:00	5:00	6:00	7:00
6	12	15	15	15	15	15	15	15	13	6			

Number	Age	Hours of each staff member
	Infants	7:00 _____ Irene _____ 3:00
5	2½-yr. olds	8:00 _____ James _____ 4:00
	Toddlers	9:30 _____ Rebecca _____ 5:30
10	Preschoolers	2:00 _____ Donna _____ 5:30
	School-agers	

Group name: 4-yr. old group (42 mos. to 60 mos.)

AM	NUMBER OF CHILDREN ENROLLED EACH HOUR												PM
6:00	7:00	8:00	9:00	10:00	11:00	12:00	1:00	2:00	3:00	4:00	5:00	6:00	7:00
	5	15	18	18	18	18	18	18	18	13	10		

Number	Age	Hours of each staff member
	Infants	Irene (children grouped together from 7-8:00 a.m. and 4:30-5:30 p.m.)
	Toddlers	8:00 Susan _____ 4:00
18	Preschoolers	8:30 _____ Deborah _____ 4:30
	School-agers	Rebecca 5:30

Group name: 5-yr. old group (60 mos. +)

AM	NUMBER OF CHILDREN ENROLLED EACH HOUR												PM
6:00	7:00	8:00	9:00	10:00	11:00	12:00	1:00	2:00	3:00	4:00	5:00	6:00	7:00
	6	12	20	20	20	20	20	20	20	12	10		

Number	Age	Hours of each staff member
	Infants	7:00 _____ Maria _____ 3:00
	Toddlers	1:00 _____ Joan _____ 5:30
20	Preschoolers	8:00 _____ Darlene _____ 4:30
	School-agers	

Staffing Pattern (continued)

GROUP OF CHILDREN	STAFFING PATTERN													

Group name

AM	NUMBER OF CHILDREN ENROLLED EACH HOUR												PM
6:00	7:00	8:00	9:00	10:00	11:00	12:00	1:00	2:00	3:00	4:00	5:00	6:00	7:00

Number	Age	Hours of each staff member
_____	Infants	
_____	Toddlers	
_____	Preschoolers	
_____	School-agers	

Group name

AM	NUMBER OF CHILDREN ENROLLED EACH HOUR												PM
6:00	7:00	8:00	9:00	10:00	11:00	12:00	1:00	2:00	3:00	4:00	5:00	6:00	7:00

Number	Age	Hours of each staff member
_____	Infants	
_____	Toddlers	
_____	Preschoolers	
_____	School-agers	

Group name

AM	NUMBER OF CHILDREN ENROLLED EACH HOUR												PM
6:00	7:00	8:00	9:00	10:00	11:00	12:00	1:00	2:00	3:00	4:00	5:00	6:00	7:00

Number	Age	Hours of each staff member
_____	Infants	
_____	Toddlers	
_____	Preschoolers	
_____	School-agers	

Group name

AM	NUMBER OF CHILDREN ENROLLED EACH HOUR												PM
6:00	7:00	8:00	9:00	10:00	11:00	12:00	1:00	2:00	3:00	4:00	5:00	6:00	7:00

Number	Age	Hours of each staff member
_____	Infants	
_____	Toddlers	
_____	Preschoolers	
_____	School-agers	

Group name

AM	NUMBER OF CHILDREN ENROLLED EACH HOUR												PM
6:00	7:00	8:00	9:00	10:00	11:00	12:00	1:00	2:00	3:00	4:00	5:00	6:00	7:00

Number	Age	Hours of each staff member
_____	Infants	
_____	Toddlers	
_____	Preschoolers	
_____	School-agers	

Staffing Pattern (continued)

GROUP OF CHILDREN	STAFFING PATTERN													

Group name

AM	NUMBER OF CHILDREN ENROLLED EACH HOUR												PM
6:00	7:00	8:00	9:00	10:00	11:00	12:00	1:00	2:00	3:00	4:00	5:00	6:00	7:00

Number	Age
_____	Infants
_____	Toddlers
_____	Preschoolers
_____	School-agers

Hours of each staff member

Group name

AM	NUMBER OF CHILDREN ENROLLED EACH HOUR												PM
6:00	7:00	8:00	9:00	10:00	11:00	12:00	1:00	2:00	3:00	4:00	5:00	6:00	7:00

Number	Age
_____	Infants
_____	Toddlers
_____	Preschoolers
_____	School-agers

Hours of each staff member

Group name

AM	NUMBER OF CHILDREN ENROLLED EACH HOUR												PM
6:00	7:00	8:00	9:00	10:00	11:00	12:00	1:00	2:00	3:00	4:00	5:00	6:00	7:00

Number	Age
_____	Infants
_____	Toddlers
_____	Preschoolers
_____	School-agers

Hours of each staff member

Group name

AM	NUMBER OF CHILDREN ENROLLED EACH HOUR												PM
6:00	7:00	8:00	9:00	10:00	11:00	12:00	1:00	2:00	3:00	4:00	5:00	6:00	7:00

Number	Age
_____	Infants
_____	Toddlers
_____	Preschoolers
_____	School-agers

Hours of each staff member

Group name

AM	NUMBER OF CHILDREN ENROLLED EACH HOUR												PM
6:00	7:00	8:00	9:00	10:00	11:00	12:00	1:00	2:00	3:00	4:00	5:00	6:00	7:00

Number	Age
_____	Infants
_____	Toddlers
_____	Preschoolers
_____	School-agers

Hours of each staff member

11. Staff Qualifications—complete the chart below for each staff member who works directly with children and for all administrators. Check the highest level achieved in formal education and Early Childhood training. Check all credentials completed. An ECE/CD unit = 16 classroom hours or 1 semester hour of study in Early Childhood Education or Child Development. ECE/CD units may be earned through college level courses, vocational courses, or other forms of in-service training.

Staff Qualifications

	STAFF MEMBERS					
Staff member and job title (use initials or first name only)	Jane Director	Joan Teacher	Donna Teacher	Irene Teacher	James Teacher	Rebecca Asst. Teacher
Years of relevant experience	10	5	4	2	2	1
Date of employment in this program	1980	1982	1983	1983	1983	1984
Formal education completed						
Some high school						
High school graduate						✓
Some college		✓		✓		
College graduate (specify major)	Early Childhood		Psychology		Elementary Educ.	
Early childhood training completed 1–6 units in ECE/CD						
7–12 units in ECE/CD						
13 or more units in ECE/CD (specify number)			18 units		24 units	
A.A. degree in ECE/CD		✓				
B.A./B.S. degree in ECE/CD	✓					
Graduate work in ECE/CD						
Master's degree in ECE/CD						
Doctorate degree in ECE/CD						
Credentials/Certificates CDA Credential						
State Certificate in Early Childhood Education	✓					
State Certificate in Elementary Education					✓	
Other (specify the number of ECE/CD units required)						

Staff Qualifications (continued)

	STAFF MEMBERS					
Staff member and job title (use initials or first name only)	Susan Teacher	Deborah Teacher Asst.	Maria Teacher	Darlene Teacher Asst.		
Years of relevant experience	3	2	2	2		
Date of employment in this program	1984	1983	1984	1984		
Formal education completed						
Some high school						
High school graduate		✔		✔		
Some college	✔					
College graduate (specify major)			Home Ec. Family Life			
Early childhood training completed 1–6 units in ECE/CD		✔		✔		
7–12 units in ECE/CD	✔					
13 or more units in ECE/CD (specify number)						
A.A. degree in ECE/CD						
B.A./B.S. degree in ECE/CD			✔			
Graduate work in ECE/CD						
Master's degree in ECE/CD						
Doctorate degree in ECE/CD						
Credentials/Certificates CDA Credential	✔					
State Certificate in Early Childhood Education						
State Certificate in Elementary Education						
Other (specify the number of ECE/CD units required)						

Staff Qualifications (continued)

	STAFF MEMBERS					
Staff member and job title (use initials or first name only)						
Years of relevant experience						
Date of employment in this program						
Formal education completed						
Some high school						
High school graduate						
Some college						
College graduate (specify major)						
Early childhood training completed 1–6 units in ECE/CD						
7–12 units in ECE/CD						
13 or more units in ECE/CD (specify number)						
A.A. degree in ECE/CD						
B.A./B.S. degree in ECE/CD						
Graduate work in ECE/CD						
Master's degree in ECE/CD						
Doctorate degree in ECE/CD						
Credentials/Certificates CDA Credential						
State Certificate in Early Childhood Education						
State Certificate in Elementary Education						
Other (specify the number of ECE/CD units required)						

List of Documents required by the Criteria

Below is a list of the written documents that are required by the Criteria with the appropriate criterion reference numbers. This list is provided to help the director evaluate those criteria and also to organize for the validation visit. Because these documents will need to be available for the validators to see, the documents either should be collected in a central place or their location should be noted in the space provided. If the information is not available on site, the director provides certification by an authorized agency or individual of the documents' existence and location.

DOCUMENT(S)	CRITERION	LOCATION
License—current certificate with date. (If no license required, provide evidence. If exempt from licensing, provide evidence of exemption and prepare a statement of voluntary compliance with state's standards, indicating which standards are not met and why.)	H-1	_____
Statement of goals and philosophy of the program.	C-1	_____
Long range, written curriculum plan. (centerwide or for groups)	B-1	_____
Daily plans for individual groups. (samples only)	B-2	_____
Written daily schedules for groups. (may be posted in classrooms or collected)	B-4	_____
Written operating policies. (including hours, fees, illness, holidays)	E-2, H-4	_____
Written personnel policies. (including job descriptions, compensation, benefits, resignation and termination, grievance procedures)	E-3	_____
Evidence of nondiscriminatory hiring policies. (such as advertisement of job openings)	E-3	_____
Attendance records.	E-5	_____
Health records of staff.	E-5, H-2	_____
Health records of children. (including record of immunizations, emergency contact information, persons authorized to call for child)	E-5, H-3	_____
List of enrolled children. (to verify health records)	E-5, H-3	_____

List of Documents (cont.)

DOCUMENT(S)	CRITERION	LOCATION
Policies of board members. (if applicable)	E-6	
Records of board meetings. (if applicable)	E-5	
Financial records and budget. (for one year)	E-7	
Accident and liability insurance. (copy of policy and/or evidence of current payment such as cancelled check or receipt)	E-8	
Records of staff qualifications. (transcripts, certificates, other documentation)	D-5, E-5	
Staff training plan.	D-1e	
Confidential personnel files.	E-5, D-5, J-1	
Documentation of first-aid training.	H-10	
Medical emergency plan.	H-11	
Emergency evacuation plan. (posted in conspicuous places)	H-21	
Food inspection certificate	I-1, I-5	
Meal plans.	I-2	
Records of staff evaluation.	E-5, J-1	
Records of child assessment. (may be anecdotal records, observations of children, checklists, collections of children's work, case studies)	J-3	

Worksheet for collecting information on Staff Qualifications

Staff member name _____

Job title _____

Group staff member is assigned to _____

Hours staff member is assigned to group _____

Years of experience working with young children _____

Date of employment in this program _____

Check highest level of formal education completed

☐ Some high school   ☐ Some college

☐ High school graduate   ☐ College graduate

(specify major _____)

Check highest level of early childhood training completed

Note: An ECE/CD unit is defined as 16 classroom hours or 1 semester hour of study in Early Childhood Education or Child Development (ECE/CD). ECE/CD units may be earned through college level courses, vocational-technical courses, or other forms of in-servicing training.

☐ 1–6 units in ECE/CD   ☐ A.A. degree in ECE/CD

☐ 7–12 units in ECE/CD   ☐ B.A./B.S. degree in ECE/CD

☐ 13 or more units in ECE/CD   ☐ Graduate work in ECE/CD

   (specify number _____)

Check all credentials or certificates completed

☐ CDA Credential

☐ State Certificate in Early Childhood Education

☐ State Certificate in Elementary Education

☐ Other credential or certificate (specify and provide the number of

   (ECE/CD units required _____)

Section 5

Staff Questionnaire
Directions for use

Sample Staff Questionnaire

Sample Summary Sheet
Open-Ended Staff Survey

Staff Questionnaire

Directions for use

What is the purpose of the Staff Questionnaire?

Many of the Academy's Criteria for High Quality Early Childhood Programs relate to the quality of life experienced by the staff and the aspects of the program that help the staff to do their jobs well. The purpose of the Staff Questionnaire is to give staff members an opportunity to evaluate those criteria. This is important because the quality of life experienced by adults indirectly affects the quality of care and education provided for children. Staff members whose health is protected and who are satisfied with their jobs are more likely to express positive feelings toward children and are more likely to remain in their positions for longer periods of time.

In this section of the *Guide* you will find

(1) a copy of the Academy's Staff Questionnaire that is used in preparing the Program Description

(2) a copy of the summary sheet that is used to tabulate the results to be reported on the Program Description

(3) a sample open-ended staff survey that you may wish to use with your staff during the self-study if you have not addressed these issues previously. This survey is for your use only and is not required by the Academy.

Multiple copies of the Academy's Staff Questionnaire (on blue paper) and a clean copy of the summary sheet are sent to the program along with the *Guide*.

Who completes the Staff Questionnaire?

All staff members who work directly with children should be given an opportunity to complete the questionnaire.

How should the Staff Questionnaire be used during the self-study?

The Staff Questionnaire should be used as an aid in the evaluation process during the self-study. The questionnaire can be used in several ways depending on the individual needs of the program. If these issues have been addressed before among the staff, the questionnaire may be used to guide discussion of how the issues currently are being met. In a small program with a great deal of ongoing communication among staff, the questionnaire could be used as an interview between the director and staff members. The questionnaire also could be used to generate topics for staff meetings to provide open discussion of these issues.

In a program where there has been little previous opportunity for ongoing communication among staff and administrators, the director may wish to get more in-depth information about the staff's feelings on these issues. In this case, the director may wish to use a more open-ended staff survey such as the one provided in this *Guide* or one prepared by the staff or director. If the director is interested in candid responses, staff members should be asked to respond anonymously. Then one staff member could be asked to tabulate the results and prepare a report.

During the self-study, the staff and director should look at the criteria that relate to staff members' needs, identify areas that are strengths and areas in need of improvement, and make improvements where possible. When the program is ready to go on and seek accreditation, the Academy's Staff Questionnaire (on blue paper) is used to collect the current information that becomes part of the Program Description. Sometimes after staff complete the Staff Questionnaire, directors find that additional improvements need to be made before seeking accreditation. If so, you may make improvements and have staff complete the Questionnaire a second time (using a different color ink perhaps). The Staff Questionnaire is used to verify the director's rating on the criterion and should reflect the situation after improvements are made.

When should the Staff Questionnaire be completed?

The Staff Questionnaire is used as one source of evidence of how well the program meets certain criteria when the center is ready to seek accreditation. The Staff Questionnaire should be filled out no more than three months before the Program Description is sent to the Academy to be sure that the results represent the current situation. Once the issues have been examined during the self-study process, completing the questionnaire should take only about 30 minutes of the staff members' time. When the questionnaire is distributed a date for it to be returned should be specified or it could be completed during a staff meeting.

How are the results reported on the Program Description?

A copy of the summary sheet appears on p. 93 of the *Guide*. To complete the summary sheet, the director or staff member assigned to this task counts the number of times each criterion is rated ☐1, ☐2, or ☐3 and records the totals on the summary sheet. Then the totals are copied onto Part 3 of the Program Description in the boxes marked "Staff Questionnaire."

The Staff Questionnaire is only one part of the self-study/validation process. The questionnaire is designed to evaluate the way in which the program addresses staff needs and helps staff to do their jobs well. Staff members study other aspects of the program using the Classroom Observation.

Staff Questionnaire

This questionnaire is for staff members in an early childhood program to evaluate the aspects of the program staff know best. The letters and numbers to the left of each item refer to a specific criterion in the complete list of the Academy's Criteria for High Quality Early Childhood Programs. This is why the letters and numbers may not be in consecutive order.

Instructions

Each statement on the left side of the page is the criterion to be rated. Criteria about staff should be rated based on your own experience and knowledge. For example, **H-9a** states, "Staff know procedures for reporting child abuse." To rate this item, ask yourself, "Do I know the procedures?"

Evaluate the early childhood program in which you work by rating the degree to which each statement on the questionnaire describes your program:

1 Not met	2 Partially met	3 Fully met
The criterion is not met.	The criterion is partially met.	The criterion is completely met.
There is **little evidence** that this statement accurately describes the program.	There is **some evidence** that this statement accurately describes the program.	There is **a great deal of evidence** that this statement accurately describes the program.

Rate each criterion by circling only **one** of the numbers 1 or 2 or 3.
Explain your ratings under the "Comments" column if
  ■ the criterion is not met 1
  ■ the criterion is partially met 2
  ■ the criterion could be met another way (List the way and explain why.)

B. Curriculum

CRITERION	RATING			COMMENTS
	Not met	Partially met	Fully met	
B-1. A long range, written curriculum plan that reflects the program's philosophy and goals for children is available.	1	2	3	
B-2. Staff plan learning activities for children based on assessment of individual needs and interests.	1	2	3	

C. Staff-Parent Interaction

C-3. Staff and parents communicate about home and center childrearing practices in order to minimize potential conflicts and confusion for children.	1	2	3	
C-4a. Parents are welcome visitors in the center at all times (for example, to observe, eat lunch with a child, or volunteer to help in the classroom).	1	2	3	
C-4b. Parents and other family members are encouraged to be involved in the program in various ways.	1	2	3	

C. **Staff-Parent Interaction** *continued*

	RATING			
CRITERION	Not met	Partially met	Fully met	COMMENTS
C-5a. A verbal and/or written system is established for sharing day-to-day happenings that affect children.	1	2	3	
C-5b. Changes in a child's physical or emotional state are reported to parents regularly.	1	2	3	
C-6. Conferences are held at least once a year and at other times, as needed, to discuss children's progress, accomplishments, and difficulties at home and at the center.	1	2	3	
C-7. Parents are informed about the center's program through regular newsletters, bulletin boards, frequent notes, telephone calls, and other similar measures.	1	2	3	

D. **Staff Qualifications and Development**

CRITERION	Not met	Partially met	Fully met	COMMENTS
D-3. New staff are adequately oriented about the goals and philosophy of the center, emergency health and safety procedures, special needs of children assigned to the staff member's care, how to handle discipline and behavior in the center, and planned daily activities of the center.	1	2	3	

D. Staff Qualifications and Development *continued*

CRITERION	RATING			COMMENTS
	Not met	Partially met	Fully met	

D-4a. The center provides regular training opportunities for staff to improve skills in working with children and families. Staff are expected to take part in regular training and professional development. The training may include workshops and seminars, visits to other programs, resource materials, in-service sessions, or course work.
— Rating: 1 2 3

D-4b. Training addresses the following areas: health and safety, child growth and development, planning learning activities, guidance and discipline techniques, linkages with community services, communication and relations with families, detecting and reporting child abuse and neglect, or other areas as needed.
— Rating: 1 2 3

E. Administration

E-1. At least annually, the director and staff conduct an assessment to identify strengths and weaknesses of the program and to set program goals for the year.
— Rating: 1 2 3

E-2. The center has written policies and procedures for operating, including hours, fees, illness, holidays, and refund information.
— Rating: 1 2 3

C. Administration *continued*

CRITERION	RATING			COMMENTS
	Not met	Partially met	Fully met	
3a. The center has written personnel policies including job descriptions, compensation, benefits, resignation and termination, and grievance procedures.	1	2	3	
4. Benefits for full-time staff include at least medical insurance coverage, sick leave, annual leave, and Social Security or some other retirement plan.	1	2	3	
9. The director (or other appropriate person) is familiar with and makes appropriate use of community resources including social services; mental and physical health agencies; and educational programs such as museums, libraries, and neighborhood centers.	1	2	3	
10a. Staff and administrators communicate frequently.	1	2	3	
10b. Staff plan and consult together.	1	2	3	

E. Administration *continued*

CRITERION	RATING			COMMENTS
	Not met	Partially met	Fully met	

E-10c. Regular staff meetings are held for staff to consult on program planning, plan for individual children, and discuss working conditions (may be meetings of small group or full staff).

[1]   [2]   [3]

E-10d. Staff are provided paid planning time.

[1]   [2]   [3]

E-11. Staff are provided space and time away from children during the day. (When staff work directly with children for more than four hours, staff are provided breaks of at least 15 minutes in each four hour period.)

[1]   [2]   [3]

F. Staffing

F-1. The number of children in a group is limited to facilitate adult-child interaction and constructive activity among children. Groups of children may be age-determined or multi-age.

[1]   [2]   [3]

F-2a. Enough staff with primary responsibility for working with children are available to provide frequent personal contact, meaningful learning activities, and supervision, and to offer immediate care as needed.

[1]   [2]   [3]

F. **Staffing** *continued*

CRITERION	RATING			COMMENTS
	Not met	Partially met	Fully met	
-2b. Substitutes are provided to maintain staff-child ratios when regular staff are absent.	1	2	3	
-3a. Each staff member has primary responsibility for and develops a deeper attachment to an identified group of children.	1	2	3	
-3b. Every attempt is made to have continuity of adults who work with children, particularly infants and toddlers.	1	2	3	
-3c. Infants and toddlers spend the majority of the time interacting with the same person each day.	1	2	3	

☐ Not applicable

H. **Health and Safety**

CRITERION	RATING			COMMENTS
H-8. Staff are alert to the health of each child. Individual medical problems and accidents are recorded and reported to staff and parents.	1	2	3	

H. Health and Safety *continued*

CRITERION	RATING			COMMENTS
	Not met	Partially met	Fully met	
H-9a. Staff know procedures for reporting suspected incidents of child abuse and/or neglect.	1	2	3	
H-9b. Suspected incidents of child abuse and/or neglect by parents, staff, or other persons are reported to appropriate local agencies.	1	2	3	
H-11a. Adequate first-aid supplies are readily available.	1	2	3	
H-11b. A plan exists for dealing with medical emergencies.	1	2	3	
H-16a. Individual bedding is washed once a week and used by only one child between washings. Individual cribs, cots, or mats are washed if soiled.	1	2	3	

☐ Not applicable

CRITERION	RATING			COMMENTS
H-21a. Staff are familiar with primary and secondary evacuation routes and practice evacuation procedures monthly with children.	1	2	3	

H. Health and Safety *continued*

CRITERION	RATING			COMMENTS
	Not met	Partially met	Fully met	

H-22a. Staff are familiar with emergency procedures such as operation of fire extinguishers and procedures for severe storm warnings (where necessary).

1   2   3

J. Evaluation

J-1a. All staff are evaluated at least annually by the director or other appropriate supervisor.

1   2   3

J-1b. Results of staff evaluations are written and confidential. They are discussed privately with the staff member.

1   2   3

J-1c. Staff evaluations include classroom observation.

1   2   3

J-1d. Staff are told what they will be evaluated on in advance.

1   2   3

J. Evaluation *continued*

CRITERION	RATING			COMMENTS
	Not met	Partially met	Fully met	
J-1e. Staff have an opportunity to evaluate their own performance.	1	2	3	
J-1f. Staff training is based on the results of the evaluation.	1	2	3	
J-2. At least once a year, staff, other professionals, and parents are involved in evaluating the program's effectiveness in meeting the needs of children and parents.	1	2	3	
J-3. Individual descriptions of children's development are written and compiled as a basis for planning appropriate learning activities, as a means of facilitating optimal development of each child, and as records for use in communications with parents.	1	2	3	

Staff Questionnaire Summary Sheet

Total number of Staff Questionnaires received _____ out of _____.

CRITERION REFERENCE NUMBER	Record number of responses		
	Not met 1	Partially met 2	Fully met 3
B-1			
B-2			
C-3			
C-4a			
C-4b			
C-5a			
C-5b			
C-6			
C-7			
D-3			
D-4a			
D-4b			
E-1			
E-2			
E-3a			
E-4			
E-9			
E-10a			
E-10b			
E-10c			
E-10d			
E-11			

CRITERION REFERENCE NUMBER	Record number of responses		
	Not met 1	Partially met 2	Fully met 3
F-1			
F-2a			
F-2b			
F-3a			
F-3b			
F-3c			
H-8			
H-9a			
H-9b			
H-11a			
H-11b			
H-16a			
H-21a			
H-22a			
J-1a			
J-1b			
J-1c			
J-1d			
J-1e			
J-1f			
J-2			
J-3			

Open-Ended Staff Survey

This survey is to help staff members think about the aspects of the program that directly affect staff. The most important determinant of the quality of an early childhood program is the quality of the staff who directly care for and educate children. However, the ability of staff members to do their best is affected by how their own needs are met and the support they receive.

Directions: check the box or boxes that best describes your experience with the program.

1. How long have you been employed in this program?
☐ Less than one one year
☐ More than one year

2. Have you received a written copy of your job description?   ☐ Yes   ☐ No

3. Which of these areas are included in the program's written personnel policies?

	Included	Not included	Not needed
Description of job responsibilities	☐	☐	☐
Salary information	☐	☐	☐
Benefits	☐	☐	☐
Resignation and termination policies	☐	☐	☐
Grievance procedures (how to appeal a decision about your job status)	☐	☐	☐

What other information about your job would you like to see in writing?

4. Which of these benefits are provided for full-time employees?

	Provided	Not provided	Not needed
Paid vacation	☐	☐	☐
Sick leave	☐	☐	☐
Medical insurance	☐	☐	☐
Social Security	☐	☐	☐
Other retirement plan	☐	☐	☐

What other benefits are you provided or would you like to have provided?

5. How effective was the orientation you received for your job?

☐ Very effective   ☐ Adequate   ☐ Inadequate

6. How were these topics addressed in the orientation process?

	Effectively	Adequately	Inadequately or not addressed
Goals and philosophy of program	☐	☐	☐
Health and safety procedures and policies	☐	☐	☐
Special needs of children assigned to you	☐	☐	☐
Discipline techniques	☐	☐	☐
Daily plan of activities	☐	☐	☐

What other topics would you like to see addressed?

7. **How would you rate the quality of the communication between staff and administrators?**

   ☐ Excellent   ☐ Very good   ☐ Adequate   ☐ Needs improvement

   How could communication among staff and administrators be improved?

8. **How would you rate the quality of communication among staff members?**

   ☐ Excellent   ☐ Very good   ☐ Adequate   ☐ Needs improvement

   How could communication among staff members be improved?

9. How would you rate the communication among staff and administrators on these topics?

	Effective	Adequate	Inadequate or nonexistent
Discussion of working conditions	☐	☐	☐
Plans for individual children	☐	☐	☐
Discussion of program planning	☐	☐	☐
Evaluation of program	☐	☐	☐

What other topics would you like to see addressed among staff and administrators?

10. How would you rate these systems designed to meet your personal needs?

	Effective	Adequate	Inadequate or nonexistent
Space for storing your personal belongings	☐	☐	☐
Staff lounge or area for taking a break	☐	☐	☐
Time for breaks	☐	☐	☐

What other systems are needed?

11. How would you rate these systems designed to help you perform your job optimally?

	Effective	Adequate	Inadequate or nonexistent
Opportunities to consult with other staff	☐	☐	☐
Paid planning time	☐	☐	☐
Sufficient resources on-site	☐	☐	☐
Opportunities for in-service training	☐	☐	☐

What other systems are needed?

12. How would you rate these opportunities for in-service training to improve your professional knowledge and skills?

	Effective	Adequate	Inadequate or nonexistent
Off-site workshops/seminars	☐	☐	☐
Visits to other programs	☐	☐	☐
Access to resource materials (library)	☐	☐	☐
In-service sessions provided on-site	☐	☐	☐
College level/technical school courses	☐	☐	☐

What other opportunities are needed?

13. Comment on the effectiveness of the in-service training in which you have participated. Which forms of in-service training were most helpful to you? In what other areas would you find training helpful?

14. How frequently is your job performance evaluated?

☐ Twice a year
  or more
☐ Once a year
☐ Less than
  once a year
☐ Never

15. How would you rate these aspects of your job performance evaluation?

	Effective	Adequate	Inadequate or nonexistent
Director observes classroom	☐	☐	☐
Director discusses evaluation	☐	☐	☐
Evaluations are written and confidential	☐	☐	☐
Opportunities exist to evaluate self	☐	☐	☐

What other ways of evaluating your job performance would you like?

Section 6

Parent Questionnaire
Directions for use

Sample Parent Questionnaire

Sample Summary Sheet
Open-Ended Parent Survey

Parent Questionnaire

Directions for use

What is the purpose of the Parent Questionnaire?

Many of the Academy's Criteria for High Quality Early Childhood Programs relate to parents who have children in the program. Whenever a program serves young children, it also serves their families. The purpose of the Parent Questionnaire is to obtain information from parents about how well the program meets the criteria that directly relate to parents, such as the criteria on staff-parent interaction.

In this section of the *Guide* you will find

(1) A copy of the Academy's Parent Questionnaire and introductory letter. This questionnaire (on yellow paper) is used in preparing the Program Description.

(2) A copy of the summary sheet that is used to tabulate the results to be reported on the Program Description.

(3) A sample open-ended parent survey that you may wish to use with parents as part of your self-study. This survey is for your use only and is not required by the Academy.

Multiple copies of the Academy's Parent Questionnaire (on yellow paper) and a clean copy of the summary sheet are sent to the program with the *Guide*. The Academy's Parent Questionnaire is also available in Spanish.

How should parents be involved in the self-study?

Some of the Criteria relate directly to families. Parents are the best source of information about how well those criteria are met. It is important to remember that parents are the consumers of the service offered by an early childhood program. Parents should be seen as a valuable source of information to help identify the strengths and weaknesses of the program and to make suggestions for improvements.

There are many ways to involve parents in the self-study. You may want to survey all the parents to get as much information as possible about how well your program is meeting the needs of its clients. A sample open-ended parent survey in this section of the *Guide* is provided for that purpose, or you may wish to use a parent survey that you have developed or acquired from another source. Another way of involving parents might be to ask for volunteers for a parent committee that could interview or survey other parents or members of the community about their needs and how well they are met by the program. Parent meetings also provide good opportunities for informing parents about the program's goal of achieving accreditation and also exploring issues about quality in an open forum with parents.

During the self-study, the staff, director, and parents should look at the criteria that relate to parents' needs, identify areas that are strengths and areas in need of improvement, and make improvements where possible. When the program is ready to continue and seek accreditation, the Academy's Parent Questionnaire (on yellow paper) is distributed to parents to collect the current information that becomes part of the Program Description.

Who completes the Parent Questionnaire?

Each family that the program serves should have an opportunity to complete the questionnaire. A copy of the questionnaire appears in this section of the *Guide*. Additional questionnaires are sent separately and should be distributed to each family the program serves. The word *parent* refers to the legal custodians of the children.

When is the questionnaire completed?

The Parent Questionnaire is used as one source of evidence about how well the program meets the criteria related to parents. To ensure the results represent the current situation, the questionnaire should be distributed no more than three months before the Program Description is sent to the Academy.

The questionnaire has a brief letter of introduction. The director (or appropriate person) should fill in the name of the program and the date by which the questionnaire should be returned (usually within three days) and sign it. After the three days have passed, parents should be reminded or encouraged to complete the questionnaire if they have not done so. It should take only ten minutes of the parents' time. To improve the return rate, the questionnaire could be filled out as parents arrive to pick up their children.

How are the results reported on the Program Description?

The results of the Parent Questionnaire are recorded on the summary sheet that appears on p. 108 of the *Guide*. The summary sheet shows which items on the Parent Questionnaire relate to which Criteria. The summary sheet is used to count the responses to the questionnaire. The director (or person assigned to this task) counts the numbers of "don't know," "no," and "yes" responses and records the totals on the summary sheet. That person should also record the number of questionnaires that were returned out of the total number distributed.

The totals from the summary sheet are copied on to the Program Description in the boxes marked with the Parent Questionnaire numbers.

Parent Questionnaire 5

For example, these boxes ☐ **DK** ☐ **No** ☐ **Yes** provide space to write in the total number of parents who responded "don't know," "no," or "yes" to question 5 on the Parent Questionnaire.

What if all the questionnaires are not returned?

You should try to obtain as many of the questionnaires as possible. Probably not all the questionnaires will be returned. Report the return rate on the summary sheet and also report what efforts, if any, you made to increase the number returned. You also may wish to explain why you think some questionnaires were not returned.

Parent Questionnaire

Prepared by the National Academy of Early Childhood Programs

Dear Parents:

_____ is working
(Name of program)
toward being accredited by the National Academy of Early Childhood
Programs. The accreditation system identifies high quality child care
centers and preschool programs.

   The Academy feels that parents can provide valuable information about
the quality of their children's center. As part of the accreditation process,
all parents are being asked to fill out the questionnaire that is attached
to this letter. The questions on it are related to the standards for
accreditation.

   You may want to say more about the program, so feel free to write any
comments on the form. You do not need to sign your name. We would
be grateful if you would return the completed questionnaire to the center
by _____.
(Date)
Thank you very much for your help.

Sincerely yours,

Program Director

Please turn the page.

Parent Questionnaire

How long has your child (or children) been enrolled in this program? Check one

☐ Less than six months   ☐ One to two years
☐ Six months to one year   ☐ More than two years

How old is your child (or children) who is enrolled in this program?

_____

Directions

For each statement, circle "Yes" or "No" or "DK" for "don't know." If the statement does not apply to your child's program, write in "NA" for "not applicable."

1. The center gives information to parents about

DK   No   Yes   (a) The program's philosophy and goals for children.

DK   No   Yes   (b) Payments and refunds.

DK   No   Yes   (c) Hours the program is open and holidays and closings.

DK   No   Yes   (d) Rules about attendance of sick children.

DK   No   Yes   (e) Menus of meals and snacks given to children; or in the case of infants, times when babies are fed and what they eat.

DK   No   Yes   2. The center has a plan for helping new children to feel comfortable by either including a visit before enrolling, having a parent meeting, or gradually bringing in new children.

DK   No   Yes   3. Teachers and parents talk about how the family and center handle different aspects of childrearing such as discipline, feeding, toileting, and other important issues.

DK   No   Yes   4. Parents are welcome visitors in the center at all times.

DK   No   Yes   5. There are many ways for parents to take part in the program, such as visiting and helping in the classroom, taking field trips, joining in at parties, or sharing a meal/snack.

DK   No   Yes   6. The center has a way of informing parents about day-to-day happenings that affect children (by notes or by teachers talking with parents when children are taken to or picked up from the center).

DK   No   Yes   7. Parents are informed about injuries and any changes in children's health or eating habits that teachers notice.

DK   No   Yes   8. Parent-teacher conferences are held to discuss children's progress at least once a year (hold conferences more often if parents want them).

DK   No   Yes   9. Parents are informed about the program through newsletters, bulletin boards, frequent notes, meetings, telephone calls (when needed), or other ways.

DK   No   Yes   10. At least once a year, parents are asked to evaluate how well the program is meeting their child's needs.

DK   No   Yes   11. Personally, I feel that the teachers have a good attitude toward me and my child.

DK   No   Yes   12. Personally, I am satisfied with the care and education my child receives in this program.

Please feel free to write any comments on what you like about the program or what you would like to see changed.

Parent Questionnaire Summary Sheet

Total number of Parent Questionnaires received _____out of _____. What efforts, if any, did the center make to increase the number of questionnaires returned?

Question number on Parent Questionnaire	Criterion reference number	Number of "don't know" responses	Number of "no" responses	Number of "yes" responses	Number of "not applicable" responses
1-a	C-1a				
1-b	C-1b				
1-c	C-1b				
1-d	C-1b; H-4				
1-e	I-2a; I-2b				
2	C-2				
3	C-3				
4	C-4a				
5	C-4b				
6	C-5a				
7	C-5b; H-8				
8	C-6				
9	C-7				
10	J-2				
11	_____				
12	_____				

Open-Ended Parent Survey

_____ is collecting information about
(Name of program)
how well we are meeting the needs of children and parents. Please answer the following questions and feel
free to add any comments. You do not need to put your name on this form. Please return it by _____.
                                                                                                      (Date)
Directions: check the box or boxes that best describes your experience with this program.

1. What information have you received about the program? What information would be helpful?

	Received information	Not received but would be helpful	Not needed
Statement of program philosophy and goals	☐	☐	☐
Payment information (fees, refunds)	☐	☐	☐
Hours of operation	☐	☐	☐
Holidays, closings	☐	☐	☐
What to do when child is sick	☐	☐	☐
Transportation and pick-up arrangements	☐	☐	☐
What parents are expected to provide (such as children's food, clothing)	☐	☐	☐
Daily activities provided for children	☐	☐	☐
How discipline is handled	☐	☐	☐
Opportunities for parent involvement	☐	☐	☐

What other information about the program would be helpful?

2. Was the procedure for introducing you and your child to the program satisfactory? What could the program do to make your child's introduction easier?

3. How would you rate the communication between staff members and parents?

☐ Very good   ☐ Adequate   ☐ Needs improvement

4. Do you feel that you are kept informed about these aspects of your child's experience?

	Feel informed	Would like more information	Not needed
Changes in child's health or behavior, injuries to child	☐	☐	☐
Child's meals/snacks	☐	☐	☐
Events of child's day	☐	☐	☐
Child's developmental progress	☐	☐	☐

What other information about your child would you like?

5. How would you rate these ways of communicating with staff members?

	Effective	Needs improvement	Not needed
Personal conversation at beginning or end of day	☐	☐	☐
Written notes	☐	☐	☐
Newsletter	☐	☐	☐
Bulletin board	☐	☐	☐
Conferences	☐	☐	☐
Phone calls	☐	☐	☐

Do you need any other ways of communicating with staff members?

6. In which of the following activities have you participated or would you like to participate?

	Have participated	Would like to participate	No opportunity	Not interested
Observed classroom activities	☐	☐	☐	☐
Helped with classroom activities	☐	☐	☐	☐
Helped on field trips	☐	☐	☐	☐
Attended party or other social activity	☐	☐	☐	☐
Attended parent meeting	☐	☐	☐	☐
Assisted in fundraising or other work	☐	☐	☐	☐
Helped with program planning	☐	☐	☐	☐

In which other activities would you like to participate?

7. How do you think staff members feel about your child?

8. How do you think staff members feel about you? Do they respect your opinions? Are they open to your suggestions?

9. Are you a welcome visitor in the program?

10. What do you like best about the program?

11. What would you like to see improved in the program?

12. What else would you like to say about the quality of the program provided for you and your child?

How to Prepare Your Program Description

Information about the Program Description
Directions for completing the Program Description

Sample Program Description

Part 1—Center Profile
Part 2—Results of Classroom Observations
Part 3—Results of Administrator Report

How to Prepare Your Program Description

In this section of the *Guide,* you will find
   (1) Information about the Program Description.
   (2) Directions for completing the Program Description.
   (3) A sample copy of the Program Description form.

With the *Guide,* you are sent
   (1) A clean copy of the Program Description to fill out and return to the Academy if you decide to seek accreditation.
   (2) A copy of the Classroom Observation Summary Sheet to return to the Academy with the completed Program Description.
   (3) A return envelope for mailing.

Information about the Program Description

What is the purpose of the Program Description?

The Program Description is used for three steps in the accreditation process:
   (1) The director uses this form to describe how the program meets the Criteria.
   (2) The validator(s) uses this form, during the on-site visit, to record the results of the validation, and to verify the accuracy of the Program Description.
   (3) Commissioners use the validated Program Description to make the accreditation decision.

What information is on the Program Description?

The Program Description has three parts:

Part 1—Center Profile. The Center Profile is where the director describes the program. The Center Profile includes information about enrollment, age groups served, length of day, purpose and philosophy of the program, how the program is organized in terms of groups and staffing, and the qualifications of staff members.

Part 2—Results of Classroom Observations. Part 2 is where the director reports the center's compliance with the criteria that are assessed in each classroom using the Early Childhood Classroom Observation. In Part 2 the director reports the center's average score for each observed criterion. The form provides space for the director to make comments about how the center meets these criteria.

Part 3—Results of Administrator Report. Part 3 is where the director reports the center's compliance with the criteria that are rated for the entire center. These criteria include policies and procedures related to the overall administration of the program. Some of these criteria are also rated by staff members and parents. Part 3 of the Program Description provides space for reporting the director's rating for each administrative criterion and for reporting the responses to the Staff and Parent Questionnaires.

Why is the Program Description used in the accreditation process?

The Program Description is designed to make the reporting process as easy as possible for directors. The form is also designed to ensure that every Program Description is the same length and organized the same way. This helps validators and commissioners, and it also helps directors who do not have the time to write lengthy descriptions of how their programs meet each criterion. The Program Description is also designed to be used by a variety of programs. There may be parts of it that do not apply to your specific program.

Although the Program Description form is structured, directors should not feel limited or constrained by it. In addition to rating each item, directors should feel free to write additional comments or explanations in the space available although no comment is necessary if the criterion is rated a ③. Directors should also indicate when they feel a criterion does not apply to their program.

When is the Program Description completed?

The Program Description should be completed after the self-study is finished and the staff and director have made any improvements they wish to make. The Program Description is necessary only if the center personnel decide to continue and seek accreditation. The Program Description should be sent to the Academy as soon as the form is completed (no more than one month later). The information reported on the Program Description is what validators will verify during the on-site visit. It is important that the information be up-to-date and reflects the current situation, not what it was when the self-study began or what is planned for the future.

Who completes the Program Description?

Although the information reported on the Program Description is collected by many people, including staff and parents, one person should take responsibility for compiling all the information and completing the Program Description. That person should be the director (or the most appropriate administrator) who will also need to be available to work with the validators during the on-site visit.

Directions for completing the Program Description

In completing the Program Description, do not write in spaces that are for validation purposes. Do not use any identifying information in the Program Description, such as the program's name, your name, or staff members' names. **Write legibly and in black ink.**

How to fill out Part 1— Center Profile

1. Write the Program Code number on the form. Each center is assigned a code number by the Academy that should be used in all contacts with the Academy and should be written on the Center Profile. The center will be identified only by the code number when Commissioners consider whether to accredit the center.

2. Answer all questions on the Center Profile. Answer the questions on the Profile keeping in mind that it will be photocopied for Commission use. Please write legibly and in black ink if possible. You may need additional space to answer some of the questions, such as the program philosophy. If so, please be brief. An example of a completed Center Profile is provided on pp. 66 to 74 in Section 4 of the *Guide.*

Please note: Licensing is a prerequisite for accreditation. If your program is exempt from licensing, you should be prepared to provide evidence of that exemption, and also to write a report of your voluntary compliance with state licensing standards including which standards you do not meet and why.

3. Fill out the Staffing Pattern and Staff Qualifications charts. Examples for completing the Staffing Pattern and Staff Qualifications charts are provided in Section 4 (pp. 69–74) of the *Guide.* The Staffing Pattern presents all of the following information in one place: organization of the groups, ages of children in each group, enrollment by hour, work hours of each staff member, and ratio of staff to children for each group throughout the day. Staff members should always be identified by their first name or initial on this chart and by the same first name or initials on the Staff Qualifications chart. If your grouping system is very complicated, the Staffing Pattern may be difficult. If you feel you cannot present it on this chart, attach a copy of your own staffing pattern, but be sure to include all the same information.

Remember—information about staff-child ratios, group sizes, and how groups of children are organized is very important. The Commission must be able to grasp a clear picture of how the program is staffed.

If the center does not meet the staff-child ratios, group sizes, and/or staff qualifications that are presented in the Criteria, you can still apply for accreditation. These criteria are important predictors of quality but the

Commission will consider the program's overall compliance with the Criteria. However, the more excessive the staff-child ratios and group sizes, the less likely it is that the center will achieve accreditation.

How to fill out Part 2— Results of Classroom Observations

1. Write in the center's average rating for each criterion. After all the observations are finished and teachers and the director agree on a whole-number rating to report for each classroom, the Classroom Observation Summary Sheet is completed. Using the summary sheet, calculate the average score across classrooms for each criterion that is rated on the Early Childhood Classroom Observation. On Part 2 of the Program Description write in the average score in the box marked "average rating."

2. Comment about criteria that are not met or are exceeded. Below the average rating box is a space marked "director's comments on rating." The director should use this space to explain any criterion that is not met or is partially met, that is any criterion with an average score of 2.5 or less. You may also comment if you feel that you meet the criterion in a different way. For instance, if your program does not have its own play-ground but provides outdoor play through use of a neighboring park, explain this difference.

The director may also comment if the center does more than is required, pointing out any particular strengths of the program. If the criterion does not apply to the program, the director should check "not applicable." The right-hand side of the page is for validators only. The director should not write in these spaces.

How to fill out Part 3— Results of the Administrator Report

1. Circle the appropriate number ☐1, ☐2, *or* ☐3 *indicating your rating for each criterion,* in the space marked, "director's rating." As director, you have already thought about how your program meets these criteria using the Administrator Report during your self-study. Now rate the program based on the current situation.

2. Report the results of the Staff and Parent Questionnaires. The questionnaires are used as another source of evidence for some of the administrative criteria. The results are reported next to the appropriate criterion in the column marked "validation procedure." To fill out this column, use the summary sheets for the questionnaires. Using the Staff Questionnaire Summary Sheet, write in the total number of times each criterion is rated ☐1, ☐2, or ☐3 by staff for the criteria in the boxes marked "Staff Questionnaire." Using the Parent Questionnaire Summary Sheet, write in the total number of parents who responded either "don't know," "no," or "yes" to each item on the Parent Questionnaire. The item numbers on the Parent Questionnaire do not match the criterion numbers, but the Program Description indicates which Parent Questionnaire number to fill in on Part 3. For example,

			FOR VALIDATOR ONLY		
	DIRECTOR'S RATING		**VALIDATION PROCEDURE**		
CRITERION	Not met / Partially met / Fully met		*Staff Questionnaire C-3*		**VALIDATION DECISION**

CRITERION

C-3. Staff and parents communicate about home and center childrearing practices in order to minimize potential conflicts and confusion for children.

DIRECTOR'S RATING

Not met [1] Partially met [2] Fully met (3)

VALIDATION PROCEDURE

Staff Questionnaire C-3

0	1	5
1	2	3

Parent Questionnaire 3

0	5	45
DK	No	Yes

VALIDATION DECISION

☐ V   ☐ NV

In this case, the director circled ③, indicating that she feels the criterion is fully met. Criterion **C-3** appears on the Staff Questionnaire and was rated a ③ by five staff members and a ② by one staff member. Question 3 on the Parent Questionnaire is related to this criterion. Five parents answered "no" and forty-five answered "yes" to that question.

Do *not* throw away the original Parent and Staff Questionnaires and summary sheets. The validator will need to see these during the validation visit.

3. Comment about criteria that are partially met or not met (ratings of ② or ①) or that are exceeded. In the space marked "Director's comments on rating," you should explain any criterion that is partially met or not met. You may also explain how your program meets the criterion in a different way. For example, your teachers may not meet the specified staff qualifications, but your teachers are well-qualified for their jobs through alternate training. You should explain this difference on the Program Description. You may also wish to indicate areas where your program does more than what is required by a criterion.

Check over the Program Description before mailing it to the Academy.

Check to make sure that you have rated every criterion. If a criterion does not apply to your program, either check off or write in "NA," for "not applicable." Check to be certain that you have filled in all of the boxes marked "Staff Questionnaire" and "Parent Questionnaire." Make sure that the report reflects the current situation.

Make a copy of the Program Description before mailing it to the Academy.

You will put a lot of work into preparing your Program Description. Sometimes things become lost in the mail. You may want to make a copy for your records. Following the Commission decision, the validated Program Description will be returned to you.

Carefully read and sign the Accreditation Release Form located in the Program Description.

Using the return envelope, mail the completed Program Description with the signed release form, the Classroom Observation Summary Sheet, and your check or money order for the validation fee (made payable to NAEYC).

Mail your Program Description so it will be received in time to allow the Academy 30 working days to arrange your validation visit.

National Academy of Early Childhood Programs

Early Childhood Program Description

What is the purpose of the Program Description?

This form is used for three steps in the accreditation process:
(1) The center director uses this form to report the results of the center's self-study, describing how the program meets the Criteria.
(2) The validator(s) uses this form during the on-site visit to record the results of the validation verifying the accuracy of the Program Description.
(3) The commissioners use the validated Program Description to make the accreditation decision.

How is the Program Description organized?

The Program Description has three parts:

Part 1—Center Profile—describes the center such as the number of children enrolled, hours of operation, staffing, and the qualifications of staff members.

Part 2—Results of Classroom Observations—used by the center director to report the average rating for each criterion that is observed in individual classrooms and the director's comments about that average rating; used by the validator(s) to compare the results of her observations of a sample of classrooms with the center's ratings and to record the results of the discussion with the director of each nonvalidated criterion.

Part 3—Results of Administrator Report—used by the center director to report the center's compliance with those criteria that are assessed through the Administrator Report, the Staff Questionnaire, and/or the Parent Questionnaire; used by the validator(s) to compare the sources of evidence to validate the accuracy of the report and to record the results of the discussion with the director of each nonvalidated criterion.

Note to director and validator(s):

Please write legibly and in black ink.

Program Code

Early Childhood Program Description
Part 1—Center Profile

Program identification—This page is removed before the Commission considers the Program Description. Identifying information about the program should appear only on this page so the Commission cannot identify the individual program.

Name of program _____

Name and title of person completing this form _____

_____

Name and title of person legally responsible for administration of program (if different from above)

_____

_____

Location of program

Street _____

City _____ State _____ ZIP _____

Phone (_____) _____

To be completed during on-site visit

Validator(s) _____

_____

Date of validation visit _____

Program Code

Note to director and validator(s): Throughout the Program Description, do not identify the program by name. Do not use full names of anyone connected with the program. Identify staff by initials or first name only.

Early Childhood Program Description
Part 1—Center Profile

1. How long has the program been operating at this site? _____
(years/months)

2. Does the program currently meet local licensing regulations?

   If yes, by what agencies is the center licensed? _____

   _____

   If no, explain _____

   _____

3. Describe the hours of operation of the program. _____

   Days per week _____ Months per year _____
(specify months if less than 12)

4. What funding sources support the program?
   Provide estimated percentage of funding received from each source.

   _____ Parent tuition   _____ Church contributions

   _____ Public funds (federal/state)   _____ Employer contributions

   _____ Community funds (United Way, etc.) _____ Other (please specify below)

   _____

   _____

5. If the program has a governing board or policy or advisory group, describe the composition of the group and its function.

6. What is the purpose of the program? (Describe the type of program, for example, a full-day child care center, half-day preschool, parent cooperative, Head Start, Montessori school, etc.)

7. What is the philosophy of the program? (**Provide a brief description of the program's goals and objectives for children. Use the space below or attach additional sheets if necessary. If you attach additional information, please be brief and also be sure the additional information does not identify the name or location of the program.**)

8. What is the total number of children enrolled in the center? _____

   Daily enrollment (if different from total above)   _____ Monday _____ Tuesday _____ Wednesday

   _____ Thursday _____ Friday _____ Saturday _____ Sunday

9. Provide the number of children enrolled by developmental level.

   _____ Infants (birth through 12 months)

   _____ Toddlers (13 months to 35 months)

   _____ Preschoolers (three- through five-year-olds)

   _____ School-agers (six-year-olds and older)

10. Staffing Pattern—use the following chart to describe how the program is staffed. For each hour of the day indicate the number of children enrolled in the group, the staff members assigned to the group (use initials or first names only), and the hours worked by the staff members. A *group* is the number of children assigned to a staff member or team of staff members occupying an individual classroom or well-defined space within a larger room. (See the example below and on p. 69 of the *Guide.*)

Staffing Pattern

GROUP OF CHILDREN	STAFFING PATTERN

Group name
3-yr. old group
(30 mos. to 48 mos.)

AM		NUMBER OF CHILDREN ENROLLED EACH HOUR											PM
6:00	7:00	8:00	9:00	10:00	11:00	12:00	1:00	2:00	3:00	4:00	5:00	6:00	7:00
6	12	15	15	16	15	15	15	15	15	13	6		

Number	Age
_____	Infants
5	2½-yr. olds / Toddlers
10	Preschoolers
_____	School-agers

Hours of each staff member

7:00 ———————— Irene ———————— 3:00
  8:00 ———————— James ———————— 4:00
    9:30 ———————— Rebecca ———————— 5:30
          2:00 ———— Donna ———— 5:30

Group name

AM		NUMBER OF CHILDREN ENROLLED EACH HOUR											PM
6:00	7:00	8:00	9:00	10:00	11:00	12:00	1:00	2:00	3:00	4:00	5:00	6:00	7:00

Number	Age
_____	Infants
_____	Toddlers
_____	Preschoolers
_____	School-agers

Hours of each staff member

Group name

AM		NUMBER OF CHILDREN ENROLLED EACH HOUR											PM
6:00	7:00	8:00	9:00	10:00	11:00	12:00	1:00	2:00	3:00	4:00	5:00	6:00	7:00

Number	Age
_____	Infants
_____	Toddlers
_____	Preschoolers
_____	School-agers

Hours of each staff member

Group name

AM		NUMBER OF CHILDREN ENROLLED EACH HOUR											PM
6:00	7:00	8:00	9:00	10:00	11:00	12:00	1:00	2:00	3:00	4:00	5:00	6:00	7:00

Number	Age
_____	Infants
_____	Toddlers
_____	Preschoolers
_____	School-agers

Hours of each staff member

Staffing Pattern (continued)

GROUP OF CHILDREN	STAFFING PATTERN													

Group name

AM	NUMBER OF CHILDREN ENROLLED EACH HOUR												PM
6:00	7:00	8:00	9:00	10:00	11:00	12:00	1:00	2:00	3:00	4:00	5:00	6:00	7:00

Number	Age	Hours of each staff member
_____	Infants	
_____	Toddlers	
_____	Preschoolers	
_____	School-agers	

Group name

AM	NUMBER OF CHILDREN ENROLLED EACH HOUR												PM
6:00	7:00	8:00	9:00	10:00	11:00	12:00	1:00	2:00	3:00	4:00	5:00	6:00	7:00

Number	Age	Hours of each staff member
_____	Infants	
_____	Toddlers	
_____	Preschoolers	
_____	School-agers	

Group name

AM	NUMBER OF CHILDREN ENROLLED EACH HOUR												PM
6:00	7:00	8:00	9:00	10:00	11:00	12:00	1:00	2:00	3:00	4:00	5:00	6:00	7:00

Number	Age	Hours of each staff member
_____	Infants	
_____	Toddlers	
_____	Preschoolers	
_____	School-agers	

Group name

AM	NUMBER OF CHILDREN ENROLLED EACH HOUR												PM
6:00	7:00	8:00	9:00	10:00	11:00	12:00	1:00	2:00	3:00	4:00	5:00	6:00	7:00

Number	Age	Hours of each staff member
_____	Infants	
_____	Toddlers	
_____	Preschoolers	
_____	School-agers	

Group name

AM	NUMBER OF CHILDREN ENROLLED EACH HOUR												PM
6:00	7:00	8:00	9:00	10:00	11:00	12:00	1:00	2:00	3:00	4:00	5:00	6:00	7:00

Number	Age	Hours of each staff member
_____	Infants	
_____	Toddlers	
_____	Preschoolers	
_____	School-agers	

Staffing Pattern (continued)

GROUP OF CHILDREN		STAFFING PATTERN													

Group name

AM	NUMBER OF CHILDREN ENROLLED EACH HOUR													PM
6:00	7:00	8:00	9:00	10:00	11:00	12:00	1:00	2:00	3:00	4:00	5:00	6:00	7:00

Number	Age	Hours of each staff member
_____	Infants	
_____	Toddlers	
_____	Preschoolers	
_____	School-agers	

Group name

AM	NUMBER OF CHILDREN ENROLLED EACH HOUR													PM
6:00	7:00	8:00	9:00	10:00	11:00	12:00	1:00	2:00	3:00	4:00	5:00	6:00	7:00

Number	Age	Hours of each staff member
_____	Infants	
_____	Toddlers	
_____	Preschoolers	
_____	School-agers	

Group name

AM	NUMBER OF CHILDREN ENROLLED EACH HOUR													PM
6:00	7:00	8:00	9:00	10:00	11:00	12:00	1:00	2:00	3:00	4:00	5:00	6:00	7:00

Number	Age	Hours of each staff member
_____	Infants	
_____	Toddlers	
_____	Preschoolers	
_____	School-agers	

Group name

AM	NUMBER OF CHILDREN ENROLLED EACH HOUR													PM
6:00	7:00	8:00	9:00	10:00	11:00	12:00	1:00	2:00	3:00	4:00	5:00	6:00	7:00

Number	Age	Hours of each staff member
_____	Infants	
_____	Toddlers	
_____	Preschoolers	
_____	School-agers	

Group name

AM	NUMBER OF CHILDREN ENROLLED EACH HOUR													PM
6:00	7:00	8:00	9:00	10:00	11:00	12:00	1:00	2:00	3:00	4:00	5:00	6:00	7:00

Number	Age	Hours of each staff member
_____	Infants	
_____	Toddlers	
_____	Preschoolers	
_____	School-agers	

11. Staff Qualifications—complete the chart below for each staff member who works directly with children and for all administrators. Check the highest level achieved in formal education and Early Childhood training. Check all credentials completed. An ECE/CD unit = 16 classroom hours or 1 semester hour of study in Early Childhood Education or Child Development. ECE/CD units may be earned through college level courses, vocational courses, or other forms of in-service training. (**See the examples on pp. 72–73 in** the *Guide.*)

Staff Qualifications

	STAFF MEMBERS				
Staff member (use initials or first name only)					
Job title					
Years of relevant experience					
Date of employment in this program					
Formal education completed Some high school					
High school graduate					
Some college					
College graduate (specify major)					
Early childhood training completed 1–6 units in ECE/CD					
7–12 units in ECE/CD					
13 or more units in ECE/CD (specify number)					
A.A. degree in ECE/CD					
B.A./B.S. degree in ECE/CD					
Graduate work in ECE/CD					
Master's degree in ECE/CD					
Doctorate degree in ECE/CD					
Credentials/Certificates CDA Credential					
State Certificate in Early Childhood Education					
State Certificate in Elementary Education					
Other (specify the number of ECE/CD units required)					

Staff Qualifications (continued)

	STAFF MEMBERS					
Staff member (use initials or first name only)						
Job title						
Years of relevant experience						
Date of employment in this program						
Formal education completed Some high school						
High school graduate						
Some college						
College graduate (specify major)						
Early childhood training completed 1–6 units in ECE/CD						
7–12 units in ECE/CD						
13 or more units in ECE/CD (specify number)						
A.A. degree in ECE/CD						
B.A./B.S. degree in ECE/CD						
Graduate work in ECE/CD						
Master's degree in ECE/CD						
Doctorate degree in ECE/CD						
Credentials/Certificates CDA Credential						
State Certificate in Early Childhood Education						
State Certificate in Elementary Education						
Other (specify the number of ECE/CD units required)						

Staff Qualifications (continued)

	STAFF MEMBERS					
Staff member (use initials or first name only)						
Job title						
Years of relevant experience						
Date of employment in this program						
Formal education completed Some high school						
High school graduate						
Some college						
College graduate (specify major)						
Early childhood training completed 1–6 units in ECE/CD						
7–12 units in ECE/CD						
13 or more units in ECE/CD (specify number)						
A.A. degree in ECE/CD						
B.A./B.S. degree in ECE/CD						
Graduate work in ECE/CD						
Master's degree in ECE/CD						
Doctorate degree in ECE/CD						
Credentials/Certificates CDA Credential						
State Certificate in Early Childhood Education						
State Certificate in Elementary Education						
Other (specify the number of ECE/CD units required)						

Early Childhood Program Description

Part 2—Results of Classroom Observations

How is Part 2 used in the center?

Part 2 is used to report how well the center meets the criteria that are observed in each individual classroom or group of children. These criteria are related to Interactions among Staff and Children, Curriculum, Physical Environment, and Health and Safety.

Each classroom is observed and rated by the teacher and director. They come to an agreement about the rating for each criterion. Then the ratings of all classrooms are averaged to determine the center's rating for each observable criterion. The average rating is reported on this form. The director may comment about the center's compliance with any criterion. **If the center does not meet or only partially meets a criterion (with an average of 2.5 or less), the director should provide a written explanation or comment. If the center exceeds a criterion, the director should also comment. The Classroom Observation Summary Sheet is sent to the Academy along with the Program Description to be used by the validator(s).**

How is Part 2 validated?

The validator observes and rates a sample of the classrooms in the center. In small centers, all classrooms may be observed. Using the space provided on this form, the validator compares her ratings of individual classrooms with the ratings reported by the center. Using the decision rules below, the validator decides if the criterion is validated **(V)**. For all non-validated criteria **(NV)**, the validator records the director's comments on this form.

Decision rules for validating observable criteria:

(1) If one or two classrooms are rated, the center's reported ratings and the validator's ratings must agree for that criterion to be validated **(V)**.

(2) If three or more classrooms are rated, there can be no more than one case of a one-point difference and there can be no cases of a two-point difference for that criterion to be validated **(V)**.

A. Interactions among Staff and Children

CRITERION

A-1. **Staff interact frequently with children showing affection and respect.**

☐ Staff interact nonverbally by smiling, touching, holding.

☐ Staff talk with individual children during routines (arriving/departing, eating) and activities.

AVERAGE RATING

C	V	C	V	C	V	C	V	C	V	C	V	C	V

VALIDATION DECISION ☐ V ☐ NV

Director's comments on rating _____

For validator _____

_____ _____

_____ _____

_____ _____

_____ _____

A-2. **Staff are responsive to children.**

☐ Quickly comfort infants in distress.

☐ Reassure crying toddlers.

☐ Listen to children with attention and respect.

☐ Respond to children's questions and requests.

AVERAGE RATING

C	V	C	V	C	V	C	V	C	V	C	V	C	V

VALIDATION DECISION ☐ V ☐ NV

Director's comments on rating _____

For validator _____

_____ _____

_____ _____

_____ _____

_____ _____

A-3a. **Staff speak with children in a friendly, courteous manner.**

☐ Speak with individual children often.

☐ Speak with children at their eye level.

☐ Call children by name.

AVERAGE RATING

C	V	C	V	C	V	C	V	C	V	C	V	C	V

VALIDATION DECISION ☐ V ☐ NV

Director's comments on rating _____

For validator _____

_____ _____

_____ _____

_____ _____

_____ _____

A. Interactions among Staff and Children *continued*

CRITERION

A-3b. Staff talk with individual children, and encourage children of all ages to use language.

For example:

Repeat infants' sounds, talk about things toddlers see, help two-year-olds name things, ask preschoolers open-ended questions, provide opportunities for school-agers to talk about their day.

AVERAGE RATING

GROUPS

C	V	C	V	C	V	C	V	C	V	C	V	C	V

VALIDATION DECISION ☐ V ☐ NV

Director's comments on rating _____

For validator _____

A-4a. Staff treat children of all races, religions, and cultures equally with respect and consideration.

AVERAGE RATING

C	V	C	V	C	V	C	V	C	V	C	V	C	V

VALIDATION DECISION ☐ V ☐ NV

Director's comments on rating _____

For validator _____

A-4b. Staff provide children of both sexes with equal opportunities to take part in all activities.

AVERAGE RATING

C	V	C	V	C	V	C	V	C	V	C	V	C	V

VALIDATION DECISION ☐ V ☐ NV

Director's comments on rating _____

For validator _____

A. Interactions among Staff and Children *continued*

CRITERION

A-5. Staff encourage independence in children as they are ready.

For example:

Infants: finger feeding self.
Toddlers: washing hands, selecting own toys.
Threes and fours: dressing, picking up toys.
Fives: setting table, cleaning, acquiring self-help skills.
School-agers: performing responsible jobs, participating in community activities.

AVERAGE RATING

C	V	C	V	C	V	C	V	C	V	C	V	C	V

GROUPS

VALIDATION DECISION ☐ V ☐ NV

Director's comments on rating _____

For validator _____

A-6a. Staff use positive approaches to help children behave constructively.

Guidance methods include

☐ Redirection.
☐ Planning ahead to prevent problems.
☐ Positive reinforcement and encouragement.
☐ Consistent, clear rules explained to children.

AVERAGE RATING

C	V	C	V	C	V	C	V	C	V	C	V	C	V

VALIDATION DECISION ☐ V ☐ NV

Director's comments on rating _____

For validator _____

A-6b. Staff do *not* use physical punishment or other negative discipline methods that hurt, frighten, or humiliate children.

AVERAGE RATING

C	V	C	V	C	V	C	V	C	V	C	V	C	V

VALIDATION DECISION ☐ V ☐ NV

Director's comments on rating _____

For validator _____

A. Interactions among Staff and Children *continued*

CRITERION

A-7. Overall sound of group is pleasant most of the time.

For example:

Happy laughter, excitement, busy activity, relaxed talking.
Adult voices that do not dominate.

AVERAGE RATING

							GROUPS						
C	V	C	V	C	V	C	V	C	V	C	V	C	V

VALIDATION DECISION   ☐ V   ☐ NV

Director's comments on rating _____

For validator _____

_____   _____

_____   _____

_____   _____

_____   _____

A-8a. Children are generally comfortable, relaxed, and happy, and involved in play and other activities.

AVERAGE RATING

C	V	C	V	C	V	C	V	C	V	C	V	C	V

VALIDATION DECISION   ☐ V   ☐ NV

Director's comments on rating _____

For validator _____

_____   _____

_____   _____

_____   _____

_____   _____

A-8b. Staff help children deal with anger, sadness, and frustration.

AVERAGE RATING

C	V	C	V	C	V	C	V	C	V	C	V	C	V

VALIDATION DECISION   ☐ V   ☐ NV

Director's comments on rating _____

For validator _____

_____   _____

_____   _____

_____   _____

_____   _____

A. Interactions among Staff and Children *continued*

CRITERION

GROUPS

C	V	C	V	C	V	C	V	C	V	C	V	C	V

A-9. **Staff encourage prosocial behaviors in children such as cooperating, helping, taking turns, talking to solve problems.**

AVERAGE RATING

☐ Adults model the desired behaviors.

☐ Adults praise prosocial behaviors.

VALIDATION DECISION   ☐ V   ☐ NV

Director's comments on rating _____

For validator _____

A-10. **Staff expectations of children's social behavior are developmentally appropriate.**

AVERAGE RATING

C	V	C	V	C	V	C	V	C	V	C	V	C	V

VALIDATION DECISION   ☐ V   ☐ NV

For example:

Two pieces of the same equipment are available so toddlers are not forced to share too often.

Preschoolers are encouraged to cooperate in small groups.

School-agers have opportunities to participate in group games or to work or play alone.

Director's comments on rating _____

For validator _____

A-11. **Children are encouraged to talk about feelings and ideas instead of solving problems with force.**

AVERAGE RATING

C	V	C	V	C	V	C	V	C	V	C	V	C	V

VALIDATION DECISION   ☐ V   ☐ NV

For example:

Adults supply appropriate words for infants and toddlers to help them learn ways to get along in a group.

Adults discuss alternative solutions with children two years and older.

Director's comments on rating _____

For validator _____

B. Curriculum

CRITERION

B-3a. Modifications are made in the environment, schedule, and activities to meet child's special needs.

For example:

Indoor and outdoor environments are accessible to special needs child including ramps, bathroom, and playground access as needed.

Schedule is modified as needed, such as shorter day or alternative activities.

Program is modified as needed, such as provision of special materials and equipment, use of supportive services, individualization of activity.

AVERAGE RATING

Director's comments on rating _____

GROUPS

C	V	C	V	C	V	C	V	C	V	C	V	C	V

VALIDATION DECISION ☐ V ☐ NV

For validator _____

B-4a. The daily schedule provides a balance of indoor/outdoor activities.

AVERAGE RATING

Director's comments on rating _____

C	V	C	V	C	V	C	V	C	V	C	V	C	V

VALIDATION DECISION ☐ V ☐ NV

For validator _____

B-4b. The daily schedule provides a balance of quiet/active activities.

AVERAGE RATING

Director's comments on rating _____

C	V	C	V	C	V	C	V	C	V	C	V	C	V

VALIDATION DECISION ☐ V ☐ NV

For validator _____

B. Curriculum *continued*

CRITERION

B-4c. The daily schedule provides a balance of individual/small group/ large group activities.

AVERAGE RATING

GROUPS

C	V	C	V	C	V	C	V	C	V	C	V	C	V

VALIDATION DECISION ☐ V ☐ NV

Director's comments on rating _____

For validator _____

B-4d. The daily schedule provides a balance of large muscle/small muscle activities.

AVERAGE RATING

C	V	C	V	C	V	C	V	C	V	C	V	C	V

VALIDATION DECISION ☐ V ☐ NV

Director's comments on rating _____

For validator _____

B-4e. The daily schedule provides a balance of child initiated/staff initiated activities.

AVERAGE RATING

C	V	C	V	C	V	C	V	C	V	C	V	C	V

VALIDATION DECISION ☐ V ☐ NV

Director's comments on rating _____

For validator _____

B. Curriculum *continued*

CRITERION

B-5a. **Multiracial, nonsexist, nonstereotyping pictures, dolls, books, and materials are available.**

AVERAGE RATING

					GROUPS								
C	V	C	V	C	V	C	V	C	V	C	V	C	V

VALIDATION DECISION ☐ V   ☐ NV

Director's comments on rating _____

_____

_____

_____

_____

_____

For validator _____

_____

_____

_____

_____

_____

(Rate only for age group being observed.)

B-5b. **Developmentally appropriate materials and equipment are available for *infants*.**

- ☐ Rattles, squeak toys, music.
- ☐ Cuddly toys.
- ☐ Teething toys.
- ☐ Mobiles, unbreakable mirrors, bright objects and pictures.
- ☐ Infant seats, crawling area, sturdy furniture to pull up self.

AVERAGE RATING

☐ Not applicable

C	V	C	V	C	V	C	V	C	V	C	V	C	V

VALIDATION DECISION ☐ V   ☐ NV

Director's comments on rating _____

_____

_____

_____

_____

For validator _____

_____

_____

_____

_____

B-5c. **Developmentally appropriate materials and equipment are available for *toddlers*.**

- ☐ Push and pull toys.
- ☐ Stacking toys, large wooden spools/beads/ cubes.
- ☐ Sturdy picture books, music.
- ☐ Pounding bench, simple puzzles.
- ☐ Play telephone, dolls, pretend toys.
- ☐ Large paper, crayons.
- ☐ Sturdy furniture to hold on to while walking.
- ☐ Sand and water toys.

AVERAGE RATING

☐ Not applicable

C	V	C	V	C	V	C	V	C	V	C	V	C	V

VALIDATION DECISION ☐ V   ☐ NV

Director's comments on rating _____

_____

_____

_____

_____

_____

_____

For validator _____

_____

_____

_____

_____

_____

_____

B. Curriculum *continued*

CRITERION

B-5d. Developmentally appropriate materials and equipment are available for *preschoolers*.

- ☐ Active play equipment for climbing and balancing.
- ☐ Unit blocks and accessories.
- ☐ Puzzles, manipulative toys.
- ☐ Picture books and records, musical instruments.
- ☐ Art materials such as finger and tempera paints, crayons, scissors, paste.
- ☐ Dramatic play materials such as dolls, dress-up clothes and props, child-sized furniture, puppets.
- ☐ Sand and water toys.

AVERAGE RATING

☐ Not applicable

Director's comments on rating _____

GROUPS													
C	V	C	V	C	V	C	V	C	V	C	V	C	V

VALIDATION DECISION　☐ V　☐ NV

For validator _____

_____

_____

_____

_____

B-5e. Developmentally appropriate materials and equipment are available for *school-agers*.

- ☐ Active play equipment and materials such as bats and balls for organized games.
- ☐ Construction materials for woodworking, blocks.
- ☐ Materials for hobby and art projects, science projects.
- ☐ Materials for dramatics, cooking.
- ☐ Books, records, musical instruments.
- ☐ Board and card games.

AVERAGE RATING

☐ Not applicable

Director's comments on rating _____

C	V	C	V	C	V	C	V	C	V	C	V	C	V

VALIDATION DECISION　☐ V　☐ NV

For validator _____

_____

_____

_____

B. Curriculum *continued*

CRITERION

B-7a. **Staff provide a variety of developmentally appropriate hands-on activities to foster positive self-concept.**

AVERAGE RATING

GROUPS													
C	V	C	V	C	V	C	V	C	V	C	V	C	V

VALIDATION DECISION ☐ V ☐ NV

Director's comments on rating _____

For validator _____

_____   _____

_____   _____

_____   _____

_____   _____

For example:

Infants/younger toddlers

Hold, pat, and touch babies for comfort and stimulation.

Talk and sing to babies.

Imitate each baby's actions and sounds.

Play mirror games, label facial features and body parts.

Allow infants to feed themselves when ready.

Encourage and support each baby's developmental achievements such as pulling up self.

Older toddlers/preschoolers

Allow time for children to talk about what they see, do, and like.

Use children's names frequently in songs, games.

Display children's work and photos of children.

Encourage children to draw pictures, tell stories about self and family.

School-agers

Provide opportunities to express growing independence/self-reliance such as the ability to make choices, initiate own activities.

Allow opportunities to work or play alone.

B-7b. **Staff provide a variety of developmentally appropriate hands-on activities to develop social skills.**

AVERAGE RATING

C	V	C	V	C	V	C	V	C	V	C	V	C	V

VALIDATION DECISION ☐ V ☐ NV

Director's comments on rating _____

For validator _____

_____   _____

_____   _____

_____   _____

_____   _____

For example:

Infants/younger toddlers

Hold, pat, and touch babies.

Talk to, sing to, and play with each baby on a one-to-one basis.

Respond to and expand on cues coming from child.

Interpret infants' actions to other children to help them get along in the group ("Mary had it first.").

Older toddlers/preschoolers

Assist toddlers in social interaction.

Create space and time for small groups of children to build blocks together or enjoy dramatic play.

Provide opportunities for sharing, caring, and helping, such as making cards for a sick child or caring for pets.

School-agers

Arrange planned and spontaneous activities in team sports, group games, interest clubs, board and card games.

Allow time to sit and talk with friend or adult.

B. Curriculum *continued*

Ratings of Center & Validator

		GROUPS												
C	V	C	V	C	V	C	V	C	V	C	V	C	V

CRITERION

B-7c. Staff provide a variety of developmentally appropriate hands-on activities to encourage children to think, reason, question, and experiment.

AVERAGE RATING

VALIDATION DECISION ☐ V ☐ NV

Director's comments on rating _____

For validator _____

_____   _____

_____   _____

_____   _____

For example:

Infants/younger toddlers

Provide a stimulating, safe environment for infants and toddlers to explore and manipulate.

Provide pictures, mobiles, brightly colored objects for babies to look at, reach for, and grasp.

Play naming and hiding games such as peek-a-boo, pat-a-cake.

Provide rattles, squeak toys, other noise-making objects for babies to hear.

Move or carry around noncrawling infants so they can see different things and people.

Older toddlers/preschoolers

Plan activities for labeling, classifying, sorting objects by shape, color, size.

Discuss daily and weekly routines in terms of time concepts, season of the year.

Observe natural events such as seeds growing, life cycle of pets.

Create opportunities to use numbers, counting objects.

Take walks around building or neighborhood.

Plan trips to provide new learning experiences for preschoolers.

Encourage water and sand play.

School-agers

Provide activities such as cooking, money-making projects, gardening, science experiments, trips in the community, interacting with visitors, multicultural experiences, computer projects.

B-7d. Staff provide a variety of developmentally appropriate hands-on activities to encourage language development.

AVERAGE RATING

C	V	C	V	C	V	C	V	C	V	C	V	C	V

VALIDATION DECISION ☐ V ☐ NV

Director's comments on rating _____

For validator _____

_____   _____

_____   _____

_____   _____

For example:

Infants/younger toddlers

Look at simple books and pictures.

Talk to, sing to, and play with babies throughout the day.

Label objects and events.

Use action rhymes.

Encourage imitation by repeating child's gestures and attempts at words.

Play verbal games, have informal conversations.

Respond to sounds infant makes.

Older toddlers/preschoolers

Read books, tell stories about experiences, talk about pictures.

Provide time for conversation, ask child questions that require more than a one-word answer.

Answer children's questions.

Add more information to what child says.

Label things in room, use written words with pictures and spoken language.

Use flannel board, puppets, songs, finger plays.

School-agers

Provide opportunities to read books.

Write and produce plays, publish newspapers, write stories.

Share experiences with friends or adults.

Use audio-visual equipment such as tape recorders.

Make own filmstrips.

B. Curriculum *continued*

CRITERION

B-7e. Staff provide a variety of developmentally appropriate hands-on activities to enhance physical development.

AVERAGE RATING

GROUPS														
C	V	C	V	C	V	C	V	C	V	C	V	C	V

VALIDATION DECISION ☐ V ☐ NV

Director's comments on rating _____

For validator _____

_____   _____

_____   _____

_____   _____

_____   _____

_____   _____

For example:

Infants/younger toddlers

Provide open carpeted space for crawling.

Provide low sturdy furniture for child to pull up self or hold on to while walking.

Provide outdoor activities for infants.

Provide objects for infants to reach for and grasp.

Allow mobile infants to move about freely, playing with and exploring the environment.

Older toddlers/preschoolers

Provide time and space for active play such as jumping, running, balancing, climbing, riding tricycles.

Provide creative movement activity using obstacle course or activity songs and records.

Provide fine-motor activities such as stacking rings, popbeads, pegboards, and puzzles for toddlers; add lacing cards and woodworking for preschoolers.

School-agers

Provide opportunities to get physical exercise, use variety of outdoor equipment.

Encourage participation in group games, individual and team sports.

Provide fine-motor activities and hobbies such as sewing, macramé, pottery, leatherwork, carpentry.

B-7f. Staff provide a variety of developmentally appropriate hands-on activities to encourage and demonstrate sound health, safety, and nutritional practices.

AVERAGE RATING

C	V	C	V	C	V	C	V	C	V	C	V	C	V

VALIDATION DECISION ☐ V ☐ NV

For example:

All ages

Cook and serve a variety of nutritious foods.

Discuss good nutrition.

Do activities to develop safety awareness in the center, home, and community.

Encourage health practices such as washing hands, brushing teeth, getting regular exercise and enough rest.

Talk about visiting doctor, dentist.

Director's comments on rating _____

For validator _____

_____   _____

_____   _____

_____   _____

_____   _____

B. Curriculum *continued*

CRITERION

B-7g. Staff provide a variety of developmentally appropriate hands-on activities to encourage creative expression and appreciation for the arts.

AVERAGE RATING

	GROUPS												
C	V	C	V	C	V	C	V	C	V	C	V	C	V

VALIDATION DECISION ☐ V   ☐ NV

Director's comments on rating _____

For validator _____

_____   _____

_____   _____

_____   _____

_____   _____

_____   _____

For example:

Infants/younger toddlers
Encourage scribbling with crayons.
Use music, records.
Sing to baby.

Older toddlers/preschoolers
Do creative art activities such as brush painting, finger painting, drawing, collage, and playdough.
Provide time and space for dancing, movement activities, creative dramatics.
Do musical activities such as singing, listening to records, playing instruments.

School-agers
Provide planned and spontaneous activities in arts and crafts such as mural and easel painting, ceramics, carpentry, weaving.
Encourage dancing, creative dramatics, record playing, singing, playing instruments.

B-7h. Staff provide a variety of developmentally appropriate hands-on activities to develop respect for cultural diversity.

AVERAGE RATING

C	V	C	V	C	V	C	V	C	V	C	V	C	V

VALIDATION DECISION ☐ V   ☐ NV

For example:

All ages
Cook and serve foods from various cultures.
Celebrate holidays of various cultures.
Read books, show pictures of various cultures.
Invite parents and other visitors to share arts, crafts, music, dress, and stories of various cultures.
Take trips to museums, cultural resources of community.

Director's comments on rating _____

For validator _____

_____   _____

_____   _____

_____   _____

_____   _____

B. Curriculum *continued*

CRITERION

	GROUPS												
C	V	C	V	C	V	C	V	C	V	C	V	C	V

B-8. **Staff provide materials and time for children to select their own activities during the day.**

☐ Infants and toddlers have some materials for free choice.

☐ Several alternative activities are available for preschooler's choice.

☐ Staff respect the child's right to not participate in some activities.

☐ Teachers pick up on activities that children start, or interests that children show.

☐ School-agers help prepare materials, plan and choose own activities most of the time.

AVERAGE RATING

VALIDATION DECISION ☐ V ☐ NV

Director's comments on rating _____

For validator _____

_____

_____

_____

_____

_____

_____

_____

_____

_____

B-9. **Staff conduct smooth and unregimented transitions between activities.**

☐ Children are told to get ready for transition ahead of time.

☐ Children are not always required to move as a group from one activity to another.

☐ The new activity is prepared before the transition from the completed activity to avoid waiting.

☐ School-age children help plan and participate in the change of activity, have time to adjust to change from school to center.

AVERAGE RATING

C	V	C	V	C	V	C	V	C	V	C	V	C	V

VALIDATION DECISION ☐ V ☐ NV

Director's comments on rating _____

For validator _____

_____

_____

_____

_____

_____

_____

B. Curriculum *continued*

CRITERION

B-10. Staff are flexible enough to change planned or routine activities.

AVERAGE RATING

	GROUPS													
C	V	C	V	C	V	C	V	C	V	C	V	C	V

VALIDATION DECISION ☐ V ☐ NV

For example:

Staff follow needs or interests of the children.

Staff adjust to changes in weather or other unexpected situations in a relaxed way without upsetting children.

Director's comments on rating _____

For validator _____

_____ _____

_____ _____

_____ _____

_____ _____

B-11. Routine tasks such as diapering, toileting, eating, dressing, and sleeping are handled in a relaxed and individual manner.

AVERAGE RATING

C	V	C	V	C	V	C	V	C	V	C	V	C	V

VALIDATION DECISION ☐ V ☐ NV

☐ Routine tasks are used as opportunities for pleasant conversation and playful interaction to bring about children's learning.

☐ Self-help skills are encouraged as children are ready.

☐ Routines are tailored to children's needs and rhythms as much as possible.

Director's comments on rating _____

For validator _____

_____ _____

_____ _____

_____ _____

For example:

Respecting infants' individual sleeping schedules, providing alternatives for preschoolers who are early risers, providing school-agers with a place to rest if they choose, respecting school-agers' increasing interest in personal grooming.

G. Physical Environment

CRITERION

Ratings of Center & Validator

G-1a. There is enough usable space indoors so children are not crowded.

AVERAGE RATING

GROUPS													
C	V	C	V	C	V	C	V	C	V	C	V	C	V

VALIDATION DECISION ☐ V ☐ NV

Director's comments on rating _____

For validator _____

_____ _____

_____ _____

_____ _____

_____ _____

_____ _____

G-1b. There is enough usable space for outdoor play for each group.

AVERAGE RATING

For example:

Age groups may use different areas or are scheduled at different times.

C	V	C	V	C	V	C	V	C	V	C	V	C	V

VALIDATION DECISION ☐ V ☐ NV

Director's comments on rating _____

For validator _____

_____ _____

_____ _____

_____ _____

_____ _____

G-2. Space is arranged to accommodate children individually, in small groups, and in a large group.

☐ There are clear pathways for children to move from one area to another without disturbing activities.

☐ Areas are organized for easy supervision by staff.

AVERAGE RATING

C	V	C	V	C	V	C	V	C	V	C	V	C	V

VALIDATION DECISION ☐ V ☐ NV

Director's comments on rating _____

For validator _____

_____ _____

_____ _____

_____ _____

_____ _____

_____ _____

G. Physical Environment *continued*

Ratings of Center & Validator

CRITERION

G-3. **Space is arranged to facilitate a variety of activities for each age group.**

		GROUPS												
C	V	C	V	C	V	C	V	C	V	C	V	C	V

VALIDATION DECISION ☐ V ☐ NV

AVERAGE RATING

☐ Nonwalkers are provided open space for crawling and protected space for play.

☐ Toddlers and preschoolers have space arranged for a variety of individual and small group activities including block building, dramatic play, art, music, science, math, manipulatives, quiet book reading.

☐ Sand and water play and woodworking are available on regular occasions.

☐ School-agers are provided separate space for their program including both active and quiet activities.

Director's comments on rating _____

For validator _____

_____

_____

_____

_____

G-4. **A variety of age-appropriate materials and equipment is available for children indoors and outdoors.**

AVERAGE RATING

C	V	C	V	C	V	C	V	C	V	C	V	C	V

VALIDATION DECISION ☐ V ☐ NV

☐ A sufficient quantity of materials and equipment is provided to avoid problems with sharing or waiting.

☐ Materials are durable and in good repair.

☐ Materials are organized consistently on low, open shelves to encourage independent use by children.

☐ Extra materials are accessible to staff to add variety to usual activity.

Director's comments on rating _____

For validator _____

_____

_____

_____

_____

G. Physical Environment *continued*

CRITERION

G-5. Individual space is provided for each child's belongings.

☐ There is a place to hang clothing.

☐ There are places for storing extra clothing and other belongings such as art work to be taken home.

AVERAGE RATING

Director's comments on rating _____

	GROUPS													
C	V	C	V	C	V	C	V	C	V	C	V	C	V

VALIDATION DECISION ☐ V ☐ NV

For validator _____

G-6. Private areas where children can play or work alone or with a friend are available indoors and outdoors.

For example:

Book corners, lofts, tunnels, or playhouses that are easy for adults to supervise.

AVERAGE RATING

Director's comments on rating _____

C	V	C	V	C	V	C	V	C	V	C	V	C	V

VALIDATION DECISION ☐ V ☐ NV

For validator _____

G-7. The environment includes soft elements.

For example:

Rugs, cushions, rocking chairs, soft furniture, soft toys, and adults who cuddle children in their laps.

AVERAGE RATING

Director's comments on rating _____

C	V	C	V	C	V	C	V	C	V	C	V	C	V

VALIDATION DECISION ☐ V ☐ NV

For validator _____

G. Physical Environment *continued*

CRITERION

G-8. **Sound-absorbing materials such as ceiling tile and rugs are used to cut down noise.**

AVERAGE RATING

GROUPS														
C	V	C	V	C	V	C	V	C	V	C	V	C	V

VALIDATION DECISION ☐ V ☐ NV

Director's comments on rating _____

For validator _____

_____ _____

_____ _____

_____ _____

_____ _____

_____ _____

G-9a. **A variety of activities can go on outdoors throughout the year.**

☐ Balance of shade and sun.

☐ Variety of surfaces such as hardtop for wheel toys, grass for rolling, sand and soil for digging.

☐ Variety of age-appropriate equipment for riding, climbing, balancing, individual playing.

AVERAGE RATING

C	V	C	V	C	V	C	V	C	V	C	V	C	V

VALIDATION DECISION ☐ V ☐ NV

Director's comments on rating _____

For validator _____

_____ _____

_____ _____

_____ _____

_____ _____

G-9b. **The outdoor play area is protected from access to streets and other dangers.**

AVERAGE RATING

C	V	C	V	C	V	C	V	C	V	C	V	C	V

VALIDATION DECISION ☐ V ☐ NV

Director's comments on rating _____

For validator _____

_____ _____

_____ _____

_____ _____

_____ _____

H. Health and Safety

CRITERION

H-7. Children are under adult supervision at all times.

For example:

Infants and toddlers are never left unattended.

Preschoolers are supervised by sight and sound.

School-agers may not be in sight, but staff know where children are and what they are doing.

AVERAGE RATING

C	V	C	V	C	V	C	V	C	V	C	V	C	V	

GROUPS

VALIDATION DECISION   ☐ V   ☐ NV

Director's comments on rating _____

For validator _____

_____

_____

_____

_____

_____

_____

_____

_____

H-12. Children are dressed appropriately for active play indoors and outdoors.

☐ Extra clothing is kept on hand.

☐ Protective clothing such as smocks and mittens is kept on hand.

AVERAGE RATING

C	V	C	V	C	V	C	V	C	V	C	V	C	V

VALIDATION DECISION   ☐ V   ☐ NV

Director's comments on rating _____

For validator _____

_____

_____

_____

_____

_____

_____

H-13a. As children use the facility, staff and children keep areas reasonably clean.

☐ Tables are washed and floors are swept after meals.

☐ Toys are picked up after use.

AVERAGE RATING

C	V	C	V	C	V	C	V	C	V	C	V	C	V

VALIDATION DECISION   ☐ V   ☐ NV

Director's comments on rating _____

For validator _____

_____

_____

_____

_____

_____

_____

H. Health and Safety *continued*

Ratings of Center & Validator

CRITERION

H-13b. Toileting and diapering areas are sanitary.

- [ ] Soiled diapers are disposed of or held for laundry in closed containers out of reach of children.
- [ ] Cover of changing table is disinfected or disposed after each use.
- [ ] Toilet area is sanitized daily.

AVERAGE RATING

	G R O U P S													
C	V	C	V	C	V	C	V	C	V	C	V	C	V

VALIDATION DECISION [ ] V [ ] NV

Director's comments on rating _____

For validator _____

H-14a. Staff wash their hands with soap and water before feeding, preparing or serving food, and after diapering or assisting children with toileting or nose wiping.

AVERAGE RATING

C	V	C	V	C	V	C	V	C	V	C	V	C	V

VALIDATION DECISION [ ] V [ ] NV

Director's comments on rating _____

For validator _____

H-14b. A sink with running hot and cold water is very close to diapering and toileting areas.

AVERAGE RATING

C	V	C	V	C	V	C	V	C	V	C	V	C	V

VALIDATION DECISION [ ] V [ ] NV

Director's comments on rating _____

For validator _____

H. Health and Safety *continued*

H-15a. **The building, play yard, and all equipment are maintained in safe, clean condition and in good repair.**

☐ No sharp edges, splinters, protruding or rusty nails, or missing parts.

AVERAGE RATING

GROUPS

C	V	C	V	C	V	C	V	C	V	C	V	C	V

VALIDATION DECISION   ☐ V   ☐ NV

Director's comments on rating _____

For validator _____

_____

_____

_____

_____

H-15b. **Infants' and toddlers' toys are large enough to prevent swallowing or choking.**

AVERAGE RATING

☐ Not applicable

C	V	C	V	C	V	C	V	C	V	C	V	C	V

VALIDATION DECISION   ☐ V   ☐ NV

Director's comments on rating _____

For validator _____

_____

_____

_____

_____

H-16b. **Sides of infants' cribs are in a locked position when cribs are occupied.**

AVERAGE RATING

☐ Not applicable

C	V	C	V	C	V	C	V	C	V	C	V	C	V

VALIDATION DECISION   ☐ V   ☐ NV

Director's comments on rating _____

For validator _____

_____

_____

_____

H. Health and Safety *continued*

CRITERION

H-17a. Toilets, drinking water, and handwashing facilities are easily accessible to children.

For example:

Facilities are either child-sized or made accessible by nonslip stools.

AVERAGE RATING

Director's comments on rating _____

C	V	C	V	C	V	C	V	C	V	C	V	C	V

VALIDATION DECISION ☐ V ☐ NV

For validator _____

H-17b. Soap and disposable towels are provided.

AVERAGE RATING

C	V	C	V	C	V	C	V	C	V	C	V	C	V

VALIDATION DECISION ☐ V ☐ NV

Director's comments on rating _____

For validator _____

H-17c. Children wash hands after toileting and before meals.

AVERAGE RATING

C	V	C	V	C	V	C	V	C	V	C	V	C	V

VALIDATION DECISION ☐ V ☐ NV

Director's comments on rating _____

For validator _____

H. Health and Safety *continued*

CRITERION

H-18a. Areas used by children are well-lighted and ventilated and kept at a comfortable temperature.

AVERAGE RATING

GROUPS													
C	V	C	V	C	V	C	V	C	V	C	V	C	V

VALIDATION DECISION ☐ V   ☐ NV

Director's comments on rating _____

For validator _____

_____ _____

_____ _____

_____ _____

_____ _____

H-18b. Electrical outlets are covered with protective caps. (NA for rooms used by school-agers only.)

AVERAGE RATING

☐ Not applicable

C	V	C	V	C	V	C	V	C	V	C	V	C	V

VALIDATION DECISION ☐ V   ☐ NV

Director's comments on rating _____

For validator _____

_____ _____

_____ _____

_____ _____

_____ _____

H-18c. Floor coverings are attached to the floor or backed with nonslip materials.

AVERAGE RATING

C	V	C	V	C	V	C	V	C	V	C	V	C	V

VALIDATION DECISION ☐ V   ☐ NV

Director's comments on rating _____

For validator _____

_____ _____

_____ _____

_____ _____

_____ _____

H. Health and Safety *continued*

Ratings of Center & Validator

CRITERION

H-19a. Cushioning materials such as mats, wood chips, or sand are used under climbing equipment, slides, and swings.

AVERAGE RATING

C	V	C	V	C	V	C	V	C	V	C	V	C	V

GROUPS

VALIDATION DECISION ☐ **V**   ☐ **NV**

Director's comments on rating _____

For validator _____

_____

_____

_____

_____

_____

_____

_____

_____

_____

_____

H-19b. Climbing equipment, swings, and large pieces of furniture are securely anchored.

AVERAGE RATING

C	V	C	V	C	V	C	V	C	V	C	V	C	V

VALIDATION DECISION ☐ **V**   ☐ **NV**

For example:

Permanent equipment outdoors, tall storage shelves indoors.

Director's comments on rating _____

For validator _____

_____

_____

_____

_____

_____

_____

_____

_____

H-20. All chemicals and potentially dangerous products such as medicines or cleaning supplies are stored in original, labeled containers in locked cabinets inaccessible to children.

AVERAGE RATING

C	V	C	V	C	V	C	V	C	V	C	V	C	V

VALIDATION DECISION ☐ **V**   ☐ **NV**

Director's comments on rating _____

For validator _____

_____

_____

_____

_____

_____

_____

_____

_____

I. Nutrition and Food Service

CRITERION

I-3. **Mealtime is a pleasant social and learning experience for children.**

☐ Infants are held and talked to while bottle fed.

☐ At least one adult sits with children during meals to provide a good role model and encourage conversation.

☐ Toddlers and preschoolers are encouraged to serve and feed themselves.

☐ Chairs, tables, and eating utensils are suitable for the size and developmental levels of the children.

AVERAGE RATING

Director's comments on rating _____

_____

_____

_____

_____

Ratings of Center & Validator

GROUPS													
C	V	C	V	C	V	C	V	C	V	C	V	C	V

VALIDATION DECISION   ☐ V   ☐ NV

For validator _____

_____

_____

_____

_____

Early Childhood Program Description

Part 3—Results of Administrator Report

How is Part 3 used in the center?

Part 3 is used to report how well the center meets all the criteria that are assessed using the Administrator Report, the Staff Questionnaire, and the Parent Questionnaire. These criteria are related to Administration, Staff Qualifications and Development, Staffing, Staff-Parent Interaction, Nutrition and Food Service, some aspects of Health and Safety, and Evaluation.

Space is provided on this form for directors to report their ratings of the center's compliance for these criteria. Space is also provided for reporting the results of the ratings supplied by staff on the Staff Questionnaire and parents on the Parent Questionnaire. Directors should comment on or explain any criteria that are not met (rating [1]) or partially met (rating [2]). **If the center exceeds a criterion, the director should also comment.**

How is Part 3 validated?

The "validation procedure" column on the form provides a code for validators. This code indicates what sources of evidence the validator will compare to validate each criterion. If the sources of evidence are consistent, the criterion is validated (**V**). If the sources are not consistent, the criterion is not validated (**NV**). The validator and director discuss all non-validated criteria and the validator records the director's comments or explanations on this form.

Validation of questionnaire summary sheets

Directions for validator

Use the original questionnaires filled out by the staff and parents and the summary sheets. Randomly select four items. Count the responses to those items on the original questionnaires to see if the totals on the summary sheets are correct. If you discover a number of errors, ask the director to redo the summary sheet(s), correct the Program Description, and initial the correction(s). Report the accuracy of the summary sheets below. If the summary sheets are accurate, move to the next step.

Staff Questionnaire Summary Sheet
- ☐ **V** (summary sheet is accurate)
- ☐ **NV** (director corrects summary sheet)

Parent Questionnaire Summary Sheet
- ☐ **V** (summary sheet is accurate)
- ☐ **NV** (director corrects summary sheet)

B. Curriculum

CRITERION

DIRECTOR'S RATING

VALIDATION PROCEDURE

Not met	Partially met	Fully met
1	2	3

B-1. A long range, written curriculum plan that reflects the program's philosophy and goals for children is available.

Staff Questionnaire B-1

1	2	3

VALIDATION DECISION

☐ V   ☐ NV

Check documents

Director's comments on rating _____

For validator _____

_____

_____

_____

_____

_____

B-2. Staff plan realistic curriculum goals for children based on assessment of individual needs and interests.

1	2	3

Staff Questionnaire B-2

1	2	3

VALIDATION DECISION

☐ V   ☐ NV

Check documents

Director's comments on rating _____

For validator _____

_____

_____

_____

_____

B-3a. Modifications are made in the environment when necessary for children with special needs.

1	2	3

☐ Not applicable

VALIDATION DECISION

☐ V   ☐ NV

Interview director; refer to Classroom Observation

Director's comments on rating _____

For validator _____

_____

_____

_____

_____

B. Curriculum *continued*

CRITERION	DIRECTOR'S RATING			VALIDATION PROCEDURE	

B-3b. Staff make appropriate professional referrals when necessary.

DIRECTOR'S RATING

Not met	Partially met	Fully met
1	2	3

Interview director

VALIDATION DECISION

☐ V   ☐ NV

Director's comments on rating _____

For validator _____

_____ _____

_____ _____

_____ _____

_____ _____

_____ _____

VALIDATION DECISION

B-4a. The written daily schedule provides a balance of indoor/outdoor activities.

1	2	3

Check documents

☐ V   ☐ NV

Director's comments on rating _____

For validator _____

_____ _____

_____ _____

_____ _____

_____ _____

VALIDATION DECISION

B-4b. The written daily schedule provides a balance of quiet/active activities.

1	2	3

Check documents

☐ V   ☐ NV

Director's comments on rating _____

For validator _____

_____ _____

_____ _____

_____ _____

_____ _____

B. Curriculum *continued*

CRITERION	DIRECTOR'S RATING	VALIDATION PROCEDURE

B-4c. The written daily schedule provides a balance of individual/small group/ large group activities.

Not met	Partially met	Fully met
1	2	3

Check documents   ☐ V   ☐ NV

Director's comments on rating _____

For validator _____

_____   _____

_____   _____

_____   _____

_____   _____

_____

B-4d. The written daily schedule provides a balance of large muscle/small muscle activities.

1	2	3

Check documents   ☐ V   ☐ NV

Director's comments on rating _____

For validator _____

_____   _____

_____   _____

_____   _____

_____

B-4e. The written daily schedule provides a balance of child initiated/staff initiated activities.

1	2	3

Check documents   ☐ V   ☐ NV

Director's comments on rating _____

For validator _____

_____   _____

_____   _____

_____   _____

_____   _____

C. Staff-Parent Interaction

DIRECTOR'S RATING

VALIDATION PROCEDURE

CRITERION

Not met	Partially met	Fully met
1	2	3

Parent Questionnaire 1-a

VALIDATION DECISION

☐ V ☐ NV

C-1a. A written description of the program's philosophy is available to parents.

DK   No   Yes

Check documents

Director's comments on rating _____

For validator _____

_____

_____

_____

_____

_____

_____

_____

_____

_____

Parent Questionnaire 1-b

VALIDATION DECISION

☐ V ☐ NV

C-1b. Written operating policies are available to parents including payments and refunds, hours, holidays, and illness.

1	2	3

Parent Questionnaire 1-c

Parent Questionnaire 1-d

DK   No   Yes

Check documents

Director's comments on rating _____

For validator _____

_____

_____

_____

_____

_____

_____

_____

_____

_____

C. Staff-Parent Interaction *continued*

CRITERION	DIRECTOR'S RATING			VALIDATION PROCEDURE

C-2. A process exists for orienting children and parents to the center that may include a pre-enrollment visit, parent orientation meeting, or gradual introduction of children to the center.

DIRECTOR'S RATING

Not met	Partially met	Fully met
1	2	3

Parent Questionnaire 2

DK	No	Yes
☐	☐	☐

VALIDATION DECISION

☐ V   ☐ NV

Director's comments on rating _____

_____

_____

_____

_____

For validator _____

_____

_____

_____

_____

C-3. Staff and parents communicate about home and center childrearing practices in order to minimize potential conflicts and confusion for children.

1	2	3

Staff Questionnaire C-3

☐	☐	☐
1	2	3

Parent Questionnaire 3

☐	☐	☐
DK	No	Yes

VALIDATION DECISION

☐ V   ☐ NV

Director's comments on rating _____

_____

_____

_____

_____

For validator _____

_____

_____

_____

_____

C. **Staff-Parent Interaction** *continued*

CRITERION	DIRECTOR'S RATING			VALIDATION PROCEDURE	

DIRECTOR'S RATING

Not met	Partially met	Fully met
1	**2**	**3**

C-4a. **Parents are welcome visitors in the center at all times (for example, to observe, eat lunch with a child, or volunteer to help in the classroom).**

Staff Questionnaire C-4a

1	2	3

VALIDATION DECISION

☐ V   ☐ NV

Parent Questionnaire 4

DK	No	Yes

Director's comments on rating _____

_____

_____

_____

_____

_____

For validator _____

_____

_____

_____

_____

1	2	3

C-4b. **Parents and other family members are encouraged to be involved in the program in various ways.**

Staff Questionnaire C-4b

1	2	3

VALIDATION DECISION

☐ V   ☐ NV

Parent Questionnaire 5

DK	No	Yes

Director's comments on rating _____

_____

_____

_____

_____

For validator _____

_____

_____

_____

_____

C. Staff-Parent Interaction *continued*

CRITERION

DIRECTOR'S RATING

VALIDATION PROCEDURE

Not met	Partially met	Fully met
1	**2**	**3**

C-5a. A verbal and/or written system is established for sharing day-to-day happenings that affect children.

Staff Questionnaire C-5a

1	2	3

VALIDATION DECISION

☐ V   ☐ NV

Parent Questionnaire 6

DK	No	Yes

Director's comments on rating _____

_____

_____

_____

_____

_____

For validator _____

_____

_____

_____

_____

Not met	Partially met	Fully met
1	2	3

C-5b. Changes in a child's physical or emotional state are reported to parents regularly.

Staff Questionnaire C-5b

1	2	3

VALIDATION DECISION

☐ V   ☐ NV

Parent Questionnaire 7

DK	No	Yes

Director's comments on rating _____

_____

_____

_____

_____

For validator _____

_____

_____

_____

_____

C. **Staff-Parent Interaction** *continued*

CRITERION

DIRECTOR'S RATING

VALIDATION PROCEDURE

Not met	Partially met	Fully met
1	2	3

C-6. **Conferences are held at least once a year and at other times, as needed, to discuss children's progress, accomplishments, and difficulties at home and at the center.**

Staff Questionnaire C-6

1	2	3

VALIDATION DECISION

☐ V   ☐ NV

Parent Questionnaire 8

DK	No	Yes

Director's comments on rating _____

For validator _____

_____

_____

_____

_____

_____

_____

_____

_____

_____

_____

C-7. **Parents are informed about the center's program through regular newsletters, bulletin boards, frequent notes, telephone calls, and other similar measures.**

1	2	3

Staff Questionnaire C-7

1	2	3

VALIDATION DECISION

☐ V   ☐ NV

Parent Questionnaire 9

DK	No	Yes

Director's comments on rating _____

For validator _____

_____

_____

_____

_____

_____

_____

_____

_____

_____

_____

D. Staff Qualifications and Development

(Refer to Staff Qualifications in Center Profile.)

CRITERION

DIRECTOR'S RATING

Not met	Partially met	Fully met
1	2	3

D-1a. Staff who work directly with children are 18 years of age or older.

Sample documents

VALIDATION DECISION

☐ V   ☐ NV

Director's comments on rating _____

_____

_____

_____

_____

For validator _____

_____

_____

_____

VALIDATION DECISION

☐ V   ☐ NV

D-1b. Early Childhood Teacher Assistants (staff who implement program activities under direct supervision) are high school graduates or the equivalent and participate in professional development programs.

1	2	3

Out of _____
(total number of)
teacher assistants,

_____ meet these
qualifications.

Sample documents

Director's comments on rating _____

_____

_____

_____

_____

_____

For validator _____

_____

_____

_____

_____

D. Staff Qualifications and Development *continued*

CRITERION	DIRECTOR'S RATING	VALIDATION PROCEDURE

D-1c. Early Childhood Associate Teachers and Early Childhood Teachers (staff who are responsible for the care and education of a group of children) have at least a CDA Credential or an A.A. degree in Early Childhood/Child Development or equivalent.

Not met [1]   Partially met [2]   Fully met [3]

Out of _____
(total number of)
teachers,

_____ meet these qualifications.

Director's comments on rating _____

_____

_____

_____

_____

_____

VALIDATION DECISION

Sample documents to verify Staff Qualifications reported in Center Profile.

☐ V   ☐ NV

For validator _____

_____

_____

_____

_____

_____

D-1d. Staff working with school-age children have training in child development, recreation, or a related field.

[1]   [2]   [3]

☐ Not applicable

Director's comments on rating _____

_____

_____

_____

_____

_____

VALIDATION DECISION

Sample documents

☐ V   ☐ NV

For validator _____

_____

_____

_____

_____

_____

D. Staff Qualifications and Development *continued*

CRITERION

DIRECTOR'S RATING

Not met	Partially met	Fully met
1	2	3

VALIDATION DECISION

D-1e. If staff members do not meet the specified qualifications, a training plan, both individualized and centerwide, has been developed and is being implemented for those staff members. Training is appropriate to the age group with which the staff member is working. *(Present training plan and evidence of ongoing, in-service training.)*

1	2	3

Sample documents

☐ V   ☐ NV

Director's comments on rating _____

For validator _____

_____ _____

_____ _____

_____ _____

_____ _____

VALIDATION DECISION

D-2a. The chief administrative officer (director or other appropriate administrator) of the center has training and/or experience in business administration.

1	2	3

Check documents

☐ V   ☐ NV

Director's comments on rating _____

For validator _____

_____ _____

_____ _____

_____ _____

_____ _____

VALIDATION DECISION

D-2b. An Early Childhood Specialist (an individual with a B.A. degree in Early Childhood Education/Child Development and at least three years of full-time teaching experience with young children and/or a graduate degree in ECE/CD) is employed to direct the educational program (may be the director or other appropriate person).

1	2	3

Check documents

☐ V   ☐ NV

Director's comments on rating _____

For validator _____

_____ _____

_____ _____

_____ _____

_____ _____

D. Staff Qualifications and Development *continued*

	DIRECTOR'S RATING			VALIDATION PROCEDURE	

CRITERION

DIRECTOR'S RATING: Not met · Partially met · Fully met

D-3. New staff are adequately oriented about the goals and philosophy of the center, emergency health and safety procedures, special needs of children assigned to the staff member's care, guidance and classroom management techniques, and planned daily activities of the center.

Director's Rating: [1] [2] [3]

Staff Questionnaire D-3 [ ]1 [ ]2 [ ]3

Interview director

VALIDATION DECISION ☐ V ☐ NV

Director's comments on rating _____

For validator _____

D-4a. The center provides regular training opportunities for staff to improve skills in working with children and families. Staff are expected to take part in regular training and professional development. The training may include workshops and seminars, visits to other programs, resource materials, in-service sessions, or course work.

Director's Rating: [1] [2] [3]

Staff Questionnaire D-4a [ ]1 [ ]2 [ ]3

Interview director

VALIDATION DECISION ☐ V ☐ NV

Director's comments on rating _____

For validator _____

D-4b. Training addresses the following areas: health and safety, child growth and development, planning learning activities, guidance and discipline techniques, linkages with community services, communication and relations with families, detecting and reporting child abuse and neglect, or other areas as needed.

Director's Rating: [1] [2] [3]

Staff Questionnaire D-4b [ ]1 [ ]2 [ ]3

Interview director

VALIDATION DECISION ☐ V ☐ NV

Director's comments on rating _____

For validator _____

D. Staff Qualifications and Development *continued*

	DIRECTOR'S RATING	VALIDATION PROCEDURE

CRITERION

	Not met	Partially met	Fully met		VALIDATION DECISION

D-5. Accurate and current records are kept of staff qualifications including transcripts, certificates, or other documentation of continuing in-service education.

Rating boxes: 1 2 3

Sample documents   ☐ V   ☐ NV

Director's comments on rating _____

For validator _____

_____   _____

_____   _____

_____   _____

_____   _____

_____   _____

E. Administration

E-1. At least annually, the director and staff conduct an assessment to identify strengths and weaknesses of the program and to set program goals for the year.

Rating boxes: 1 2 3

Staff Questionnaire E-1

Boxes: 1 2 3

VALIDATION DECISION

☐ V   ☐ NV

Director's comments on rating _____

For validator _____

_____   _____

_____   _____

_____   _____

_____   _____

E. Administration *continued*

VALIDATION PROCEDURE

CRITERION

DIRECTOR'S RATING

Not met	Partially met	Fully met
1	2	3

E-2. The center has written policies and procedures for operating, including hours, fees, illness, holidays, and refund information.

Staff Questionnaire E-2

1	2	3

VALIDATION DECISION

☐ V   ☐ NV

`Check documents

Director's comments on rating _____

For validator _____

_____

_____

_____

_____

_____

E-3a. The center has written personnel policies, including job descriptions, compensation, benefits, resignation and termination, and grievance procedures.

1	2	3

Staff Questionnaire E-3a

1	2	3

VALIDATION DECISION

☐ V   ☐ NV

Check documents

Director's comments on rating _____

For validator _____

_____

_____

_____

_____

_____

E-3b. Hiring practices are nondiscriminatory.
(Present copy of advertised position or other evidence of equal opportunity employment.)

1	2	3

Check documents

VALIDATION DECISION

☐ V   ☐ NV

Director's comments on rating _____

For validator _____

_____

_____

_____

_____

E. Administration *continued*

CRITERION

DIRECTOR'S RATING

Not met	Partially met	Fully met
1	2	3

E-4. **Benefits for full-time staff include at least medical insurance coverage, sick leave, annual leave, and Social Security or some other retirement plan.**

Staff Questionnaire E-4

1	2	3

VALIDATION DECISION

☐ V ☐ NV

Director's comments on rating _____

For validator _____

_____

_____

_____

_____

_____

E-5a. **Attendance records are kept.**

1	2	3

Check documents

VALIDATION DECISION

☐ V ☐ NV

Director's comments on rating _____

For validator _____

_____

_____

_____

_____

_____

E-5b. **Confidential personnel files are kept including résumés with record of experience, transcripts of education, documentation of in-service training, and results of performance evaluation.** (See criterion **J-1**.)

1	2	3

Sample documents

VALIDATION DECISION

☐ V ☐ NV

Director's comments on rating _____

For validator _____

_____

_____

_____

_____

_____

E. Administration *continued*

DIRECTOR'S RATING

VALIDATION PROCEDURE

CRITERION

Not met	Partially met	Fully met
1	2	3

VALIDATION DECISION

E-6a. In cases where the center is governed by a board of directors, the center has written policies defining roles and responsibilities of board members and staff.

Check documents

☐ V   ☐ NV

☐ Not applicable

Director's comments on rating _____

For validator _____

VALIDATION DECISION

E-6b. Records of board meetings (minutes) are kept.

1	2	3

Check documents

☐ V   ☐ NV

☐ Not applicable

Director's comments on rating _____

For validator _____

E. Administration *continued*

CRITERION

DIRECTOR'S RATING

Not met	Partially met	Fully met
1	2	3

VALIDATION DECISION

E-7. **Fiscal records are kept with evidence of long range budgeting and sound financial planning (projections of at least one year are needed).**

Check documents

☐ V   ☐ NV

Director's comments on rating _____

For validator _____

_____

_____

_____

_____

_____

_____

_____

_____

_____

_____

VALIDATION DECISION

E-8. **Accident protection and liability insurance coverage is maintained for children and adults.**
(Present policy and/or most recent canceled check or receipt for payment.)

1	2	3

Check documents

☐ V   ☐ NV

Director's comments on rating _____

For validator _____

_____

_____

_____

_____

_____

_____

_____

_____

_____

_____

Staff Questionnaire E-9

VALIDATION DECISION

E-9. **The director (or other appropriate person) is familiar with and makes appropriate use of community resources including social services; mental and physical health agencies; and educational programs such as museums, libraries, and neighborhood centers.**

1	2	3

1	2	3

☐ V   ☐ NV

Director's comments on rating _____

For validator _____

_____

_____

_____

_____

_____

_____

_____

_____

E. Administration *continued*

CRITERION	DIRECTOR'S RATING			VALIDATION PROCEDURE	

CRITERION

DIRECTOR'S RATING

Not met	Partially met	Fully met
1	2	3

VALIDATION PROCEDURE

E-10a. Staff and administrators communicate frequently.

Staff Questionnaire E-10a

1	2	3

VALIDATION DECISION

☐ V ☐ NV

Interview director

Director's comments on rating _____

For validator _____

_____

_____

_____

_____

E-10b. Staff plan and consult together.

1	2	3

Staff Questionnaire E-10b

1	2	3

VALIDATION DECISION

☐ V ☐ NV

Interview director

Director's comments on rating _____

For validator _____

_____

_____

_____

_____

E-10c. Regular staff meetings are held for staff to consult on program planning, plan for individual children, and discuss working conditions (may be meetings of small groups or full staff).

1	2	3

Staff Questionnaire E-10c

1	2	3

VALIDATION DECISION

☐ V ☐ NV

Interview director

Director's comments on rating _____

For validator _____

_____

_____

_____

_____

E. Administration *continued*

CRITERION

DIRECTOR'S RATING

VALIDATION PROCEDURE

Not met	Partially met	Fully met
1	2	3

E-10d. Staff are provided paid planning time.

Staff Questionnaire E-10d

1 2 3

VALIDATION DECISION

☐ V ☐ NV

Interview director

Director's comments on rating _____

For validator _____

_____

_____

_____

_____

_____

E-11. Staff are provided space and time away from children during the day. (When staff work directly with children for more than four hours, staff are provided breaks of at least 15 minutes in each four hour period.)

1	2	3

Staff Questionnaire E-11

1 2 3

VALIDATION DECISION

☐ V ☐ NV

Director's comments on rating _____

For validator _____

_____

_____

_____

_____

_____

F. Staffing

(Refer to group size and staff-child ratio information in Center Profile—Section 7, Part 1.)

F-1 and F-2. Staff-child ratios within group size

Age of children*	Group size									
	6	8	10	12	14	16	18	20	22	24
Infants (birth–12mos.)	1:3	1:4								
Toddlers (12–24 mos.)	1:3	1:4	1:5	1:4						
Two-year-olds (24–36 mos.)		1:4	1:5	1:6**						
Two- and three-year-olds			1:5	1:6	1:7**					
Three-year-olds					1:7	1:8	1:9	1:10**		
Four-year-olds						1:8	1:9	1:10**		
Four- and five-year-olds						1:8	1:9	1:10**		
Five-year-olds						1:8	1:9	1:10		
Six- to eight-year-olds (school age)								1:10	1:11	1:12

* Multi-age grouping is both permissible and desirable. When infants are not included, the staff-child ratio and group size requirements shall be based on the age of the majority of the children in the group. When infants are included, ratios and group size for infants must be maintained.

** Smaller group sizes and lower staff-child ratios are optimal. Larger group sizes and higher staff-child ratios are acceptable only in cases where staff are highly qualified (see Staff Qualifications, **D-1** and **D-2**).

CRITERION

DIRECTOR'S RATING

VALIDATION PROCEDURE

F-1. The number of children in a group is limited to facilitate adult-child interaction and constructive activity among children. Groups of children may be age-determined or multi-age. *(Using the chart above, determine which groups meet or exceed the required group sizes.)*

Not met	Partially met	Fully met
1	2	3

Out of _____ groups,
(total number of)

_____ groups meet group size requirements.

Director's comments on rating _____

_____

_____

_____

_____

Staff Questionnaire F-1

1	2	3

VALIDATION DECISION

☐ V   ☐ NV

Observe sample of classrooms and verify group sizes reported in Center Profile.

For validator _____

_____

_____

_____

F. Staffing *continued*

CRITERION	DIRECTOR'S RATING	VALIDATION PROCEDURE

F-2a. **Enough staff with primary responsibility for working with children are available to provide frequent personal contact, meaningful learning activities, and supervision, and to offer immediate care as needed.**
(Using the chart above, determine which groups meet or exceed the required staff-child ratios.)

DIRECTOR'S RATING

Not met	Partially met	Fully met
1	2	3

Out of _____ groups,
(total number of)

_____ groups meet
staff-child ratio
requirements.

Director's comments on rating _____

_____

_____

_____

_____

_____

VALIDATION PROCEDURE

Staff Questionnaire F-2a

1	2	3

VALIDATION DECISION

☐ V   ☐ NV

Observe sample of classrooms and verify staff-child ratios reported in Center Profile.

For validator _____

_____

_____

_____

_____

_____

F-2b. **Substitutes are provided to maintain staff-child ratios when regular staff are absent.**

1	2	3

Director's comments on rating _____

_____

_____

_____

_____

_____

Staff Questionnaire F-2b

1	2	3

VALIDATION DECISION

☐ V   ☐ NV

For validator _____

_____

_____

_____

_____

_____

F. Staffing *continued*

CRITERION	DIRECTOR'S RATING	VALIDATION PROCEDURE

DIRECTOR'S RATING

Not met — Partially met — Fully met

VALIDATION PROCEDURE

F-3a. Each staff member has primary responsibility for and develops a deeper attachment to an identified group of children.

Director's Rating: 1   2   3

Staff Questionnaire F-3a   1   2   3

Check Staffing Pattern

VALIDATION DECISION ☐ V ☐ NV

Director's comments on rating _____

For validator _____

F-3b. Every attempt is made to have continuity of adults who work with children, particularly infants and toddlers.

Director's Rating: 1   2   3

Staff Questionnaire F-3b   1   2   3

Check Staffing Pattern

VALIDATION DECISION ☐ V ☐ NV

Director's comments on rating _____

For validator _____

F-3c. Infants and toddlers spend the majority of the time interacting with the same person each day.

Director's Rating: 1   2   3

☐ Not applicable

Staff Questionnaire F-3c   1   2   3

Check Staffing Pattern

VALIDATION DECISION ☐ V ☐ NV

Director's comments on rating _____

For validator _____

G. Physical Environment

CRITERION

DIRECTOR'S RATING

Not met	Partially met	Fully met
1	2	3

VALIDATION DECISION

G-1a. There is a minimum of 35 square feet of usable playroom floor space per child indoors.

Observe facility

☐ V   ☐ NV

Give actual square feet if less than 35 square feet _____.

Director's comments on rating _____

For validator _____

_____   _____

_____   _____

_____   _____

_____   _____

VALIDATION DECISION

G-1b. There is a minimum of 75 square feet of play space outdoors per child (when space is in use).

| 1 | 2 | 3 |

Observe facility

☐ V   ☐ NV

Give actual square feet if less than 75 square feet _____.

Director's comments on rating _____

For validator _____

_____   _____

_____   _____

_____   _____

_____   _____

H. Health and Safety

VALIDATION DECISION

H-1. The center is licensed or accredited by the appropriate state/local agencies. If exempt from licensing, the center demonstrates compliance with its own state regulations.

| 1 | 2 | 3 |

Check license

☐ V   ☐ NV

Director's comments on rating _____

For validator _____

_____   _____

_____   _____

_____   _____

H. Health and Safety *continued*

CRITERION	DIRECTOR'S RATING			VALIDATION PROCEDURE

DIRECTOR'S RATING

Not met	Partially met	Fully met
1	2	3

H-2a. Staff health records include results of pre-employment physical, results of tuberculosis test, (within last two years) and emergency contact information.

Director's rating: [1] [2] [3]

VALIDATION DECISION

Sample documents   ☐ V   ☐ NV

Director's comments on rating _____

For validator _____

_____

_____

_____

_____

VALIDATION DECISION

H-2b. New staff members serve a probationary period during which their physical and psychological competence for working with children is evaluated.

Director's rating: [1] [2] [3]

Interview director   ☐ V   ☐ NV

Director's comments on rating _____

For validator _____

_____

_____

_____

_____

VALIDATION DECISION

H-3. Child health records include results of recent health examination, up-to-date record of immunizations, emergency contact information, names of people authorized to call for the child, and important health history (such as allergies, chronic illness).

Director's rating: [1] [2] [3]

Sample documents   ☐ V   ☐ NV

Director's comments on rating _____

For validator _____

_____

_____

_____

_____

H. Health and Safety *continued*

		DIRECTOR'S RATING		**FOR VALIDATOR ONLY**
				VALIDATION PROCEDURE

CRITERION

	Not met	Partially met	Fully met
	1	2	3

H-4. The center has a written policy specifying limitations on attendance of sick children. Provisions are made for the notification of the sick child's parents, the comfort of the child, and the protection of well children.

Parent Questionnaire 1-d

DK	No	Yes

Check documents

VALIDATION DECISION
☐ V   ☐ NV

Director's comments on rating _____

For validator _____

_____   _____

_____   _____

_____   _____

_____   _____

VALIDATION DECISION
☐ V   ☐ NV

H-5. Provisions are made for safe arrival and departure of all children that also allow for parent-staff interaction. A system exists for ensuring that children are released only to authorized people.

1	2	3

Observe arrival/departure; interview director

Director's comments on rating _____

For validator _____

_____   _____

_____   _____

_____   _____

_____   _____

VALIDATION DECISION
☐ V   ☐ NV

H-6. If transportation is provided for children by the center, vehicles are equipped with age-appropriate restraint devices, and appropriate safety precautions are taken.

1	2	3

☐ Not applicable

Interview director; observe vehicles

Director's comments on rating _____

For validator _____

_____   _____

_____   _____

_____   _____

_____   _____

H. Health and Safety *continued*

CRITERION	DIRECTOR'S RATING			VALIDATION PROCEDURE

DIRECTOR'S RATING

Not met	Partially met	Fully met
1	2	3

H-8. Staff are alert to the health of each child. Individual medical problems and accidents are recorded and reported to staff and parents, and a written record is kept of such incidents.

Staff Questionnaire H-8

1	2	3

Parent Questionnaire 7

DK	No	Yes

VALIDATION DECISION

☐ V   ☐ NV

Director's comments on rating _____

_____

_____

_____

_____

_____

For validator _____

_____

_____

_____

_____

_____

H-9a. Staff know procedures for reporting suspected incidents of child abuse and/or neglect.

1	2	3

Staff Questionnaire H-9a

1	2	3

VALIDATION DECISION

☐ V   ☐ NV

Director's comments on rating _____

_____

_____

_____

_____

For validator _____

_____

_____

_____

_____

H. Health and Safety *continued*

CRITERION

DIRECTOR'S RATING

Not met	Partially met	Fully met
1	2	3

H-9b. Suspected incidents of child abuse and/or neglect by parents, staff, or other persons are reported to appropriate local agencies.

Staff Questionnaire H-9b

1	2	3

VALIDATION DECISION

☐ V   ☐ NV

Director's comments on rating _____

For validator _____

_____   _____

_____   _____

_____   _____

_____   _____

_____   _____

VALIDATION DECISION

H-10. At least one staff member who has certification in emergency first-aid treatment and CPR is always in the center. Current certificates are kept on file.

1	2	3

Check documents

☐ V   ☐ NV

Director's comments on rating _____

For validator _____

_____   _____

_____   _____

_____   _____

_____   _____

H-11a. Adequate first-aid supplies are readily available.

1	2	3

Staff Questionnaire H-11a

1	2	3

VALIDATION DECISION

☐ V   ☐ NV

Observe supplies

Director's comments on rating _____

For validator _____

_____   _____

_____   _____

_____   _____

_____   _____

H. Health and Safety *continued*

	DIRECTOR'S RATING			VALIDATION PROCEDURE

CRITERION

DIRECTOR'S RATING: Not met **1**, Partially met **2**, Fully met **3**

H-11b. A plan exists for dealing with medical emergencies that includes a source of emergency care, written parental consent forms, and transportation arrangements.

Director's rating: 1   2   3

Staff Questionnaire H-11b

1   2   3

VALIDATION DECISION
☐ V   ☐ NV

Check documents

Director's comments on rating _____

For validator _____

_____ _____

_____ _____

_____ _____

_____ _____

VALIDATION DECISION
☐ V   ☐ NV

H-13a. The facility is cleaned daily, including disinfecting bathroom fixtures and removing trash.

1   2   3

Observe facility on tour

Director's comments on rating _____

For validator _____

_____ _____

_____ _____

_____ _____

_____ _____

VALIDATION DECISION
☐ V   ☐ NV

H-13b. Infants' equipment is washed and disinfected at least twice a week. Toys that are mouthed are washed daily.

1   2   3

☐ Not applicable

Interview director

Director's comments on rating _____

For validator _____

_____ _____

_____ _____

_____ _____

_____ _____

H. Health and Safety *continued*

CRITERION

DIRECTOR'S RATING

VALIDATION PROCEDURE

Not met	Partially met	Fully met
1	2	3

H-16a. Individual bedding is washed once a week and used by only one child between washings. Individual cribs, cots, or mats are washed if soiled.

☐ Not applicable

Staff Questionnaire H-16a

☐ 1 ☐ 2 ☐ 3

VALIDATION DECISION
☐ V   ☐ NV

Director's comments on rating _____

For validator _____

H-17. Hot water does not exceed 110°F (43°C) at outlets used by children.

| 1 | 2 | 3 |

Feel water temperature

VALIDATION DECISION
☐ V   ☐ NV

Director's comments on rating _____

For validator _____

H-18d. Nontoxic building materials are used.

| 1 | 2 | 3 |

Interview director

VALIDATION DECISION
☐ V   ☐ NV

Director's comments on rating _____

For validator _____

H. Health and Safety *continued*

CRITERION | DIRECTOR'S RATING | VALIDATION PROCEDURE

H-18e. Stairways are well-lighted and equipped with handrails.

Not met [1] Partially met [2] Fully met [3]

☐ Not applicable

Director's comments on rating _____

Observe facility

VALIDATION DECISION
☐ V   ☐ NV

For validator _____

_____
_____
_____
_____
_____

H-18f. Screens are placed on all windows that open (when appropriate).

[1] [2] [3]

Observe facility

VALIDATION DECISION
☐ V   ☐ NV

Director's comments on rating _____

For validator _____

_____
_____
_____
_____
_____

H-20a. All chemicals and potentially dangerous products such as medicines or cleaning supplies are stored in original, labeled containers in locked cabinets inaccessible to children.

[1] [2] [3]

Interview director; refer to Classroom Observation

VALIDATION DECISION
☐ V   ☐ NV

Director's comments on rating _____

For validator _____

_____
_____
_____
_____

H. Health and Safety *continued*

CRITERION

DIRECTOR'S RATING

VALIDATION PROCEDURE

Not met	Partially met	Fully met
1	2	3

VALIDATION DECISION

H-20b. Medication is administered to children only when a written order is submitted by a parent, and the medication is administered by a consistently designated staff member. Written records are kept of medication given to children.

Interview director; check documents

☐ V   ☐ NV

Director's comments on rating _____

For validator _____

_____

_____

_____

_____

_____

_____

_____

_____

_____

_____

H-21a. Staff are familiar with primary and secondary evacuation routes and practice evacuation procedures monthly with children.

1	2	3

Staff Questionnaire H-21a

1	2	3

VALIDATION DECISION

☐ V   ☐ NV

Check documents

Director's comments on rating _____

For validator _____

_____

_____

_____

_____

_____

_____

_____

_____

_____

_____

H-21b. Written emergency procedures are posted in conspicuous places.

1	2	3

VALIDATION DECISION

Observe facility

☐ V   ☐ NV

Director's comments on rating _____

For validator _____

_____

_____

_____

_____

_____

_____

_____

_____

H. Health and Safety *continued*

CRITERION

DIRECTOR'S RATING

VALIDATION PROCEDURE

Not met	Partially met	Fully met
1	2	3

Staff Questionnaire H-22a

VALIDATION DECISION

☐ V   ☐ NV

H-22a. Staff are familiar with emergency procedures such as operation of fire extinguishers and procedures for severe storm warnings (where necessary).

1	2	3

Director's comments on rating _____

For validator _____

_____ _____

_____ _____

_____ _____

_____ _____

_____ _____

VALIDATION DECISION

☐ V   ☐ NV

H-22b. Smoke detectors and fire extinguishers are provided and periodically checked.

1	2	3

Observe facility

Director's comments on rating _____

For validator _____

_____ _____

_____ _____

_____ _____

_____ _____

_____ _____

VALIDATION DECISION

☐ V   ☐ NV

H-22c. Emergency telephone numbers including police, fire, rescue, and poison control services are posted by telephones.

1	2	3

Observe facility

Director's comments on rating _____

For validator _____

_____ _____

_____ _____

_____ _____

_____ _____

I. Nutrition and Food Service

CRITERION	DIRECTOR'S RATING			VALIDATION PROCEDURE

I-1. Meals and/or snacks are planned to meet the child's nutritional requirements in proportion to the amount of time the child is in the program each day, as recommended by the Child Care Food Program of the U.S. Department of Agriculture.

Director's Rating: Not met **1** | Partially met **2** | Fully met **3**

Check meal plans, current food inspection certificate

☐ V   ☐ NV

Director's comments on rating _____

_____
_____
_____
_____

For validator _____

_____
_____
_____
_____
_____

I-2a. Written menus are provided for parents.

Director's Rating: **1** | **2** | **3**

Parent Questionnaire 1-e

DK | No | Yes

Check documents

VALIDATION DECISION

☐ V   ☐ NV

Director's comments on rating _____

_____
_____
_____
_____

For validator _____

_____
_____
_____
_____

I-2b. Feeding times and food consumption information is provided to parents of infants and toddlers at the end of each day.

Director's Rating: **1** | **2** | **3**

☐ Not applicable

Parent Questionnaire 1-e

DK | No | Yes

VALIDATION DECISION

☐ V   ☐ NV

Director's comments on rating _____

_____
_____
_____
_____

For validator _____

_____
_____
_____
_____

I. Nutrition and Food Service *continued*

CRITERION	DIRECTOR'S RATING			VALIDATION PROCEDURE

DIRECTOR'S RATING

Not met — Partially met — Fully met

VALIDATION DECISION

I-3. Foods indicative of children's cultural backgrounds are served periodically.

[1] [2] [3]

Check meal plans   ☐ V   ☐ NV

Director's comments on rating _____

For validator _____

_____

_____

_____

_____

VALIDATION DECISION

I-4. Food brought from home is stored appropriately until consumed.

[1] [2] [3]

☐ Not applicable

Observe facility   ☐ V   ☐ NV

Director's comments on rating _____

For validator _____

_____

_____

_____

_____

VALIDATION DECISION

I-5. Where food is prepared on the premises, the center is in compliance with legal requirements for food preparation and service. Food may be prepared at an approved facility and transported to the program in appropriate sanitary containers and at appropriate temperatures.

[1] [2] [3]

Check current food inspection certificate   ☐ V   ☐ NV

Director's comments on rating _____

For validator _____

_____

_____

_____

_____

J. Evaluation

CRITERION

DIRECTOR'S RATING

Not met	Partially met	Fully met
1	2	3

J-1a. All staff are evaluated at least annually by the director or other appropriate supervisor.

Staff Questionnaire J-1a

| 1 | 2 | 3 |

VALIDATION DECISION

☐ V   ☐ NV

Director's comments on rating _____

For validator _____

_____

_____

_____

_____

J-1b. Results of staff evaluations are written and confidential. They are discussed privately with the staff member.

| 1 | 2 | 3 |

Staff Questionnaire J-1b

| 1 | 2 | 3 |

VALIDATION DECISION

☐ V   ☐ NV

Director's comments on rating _____

For validator _____

_____

_____

_____

_____

J-1c. Staff evaluations include classroom observation.

| 1 | 2 | 3 |

Staff Questionnaire J-1c

| 1 | 2 | 3 |

VALIDATION DECISION

☐ V   ☐ NV

Director's comments on rating _____

For validator _____

_____

_____

_____

_____

J. Evaluation *continued*

CRITERION

DIRECTOR'S RATING		
Not met	Partially met	Fully met
1	2	3

VALIDATION PROCEDURE

J-1d. Staff are informed of evaluation criteria in advance.

Staff Questionnaire J-1d

1	2	3

VALIDATION DECISION

☐ V ☐ NV

Director's comments on rating _____

For validator _____

_____

_____

_____

_____

_____

_____

_____

_____

_____

_____

J-1e. Staff have an opportunity to evaluate their own performance.

1	2	3

Staff Questionnaire J-1e

1	2	3

VALIDATION DECISION

☐ V ☐ NV

Director's comments on rating _____

For validator _____

_____

_____

_____

_____

_____

_____

_____

_____

_____

_____

J-1f. A plan for staff training is generated from the evaluation process.

1	2	3

Staff Questionnaire J-1f

1	2	3

VALIDATION DECISION

☐ V ☐ NV

Director's comments on rating _____

For validator _____

_____

_____

_____

_____

_____

_____

_____

_____

_____

_____

J. Evaluation *continued*

CRITERION

DIRECTOR'S RATING

VALIDATION PROCEDURE

Not met	Partially met	Fully met
1	2	3

J-2. At least once a year, staff, other professionals, and parents are involved in evaluating the program's effectiveness in meeting the needs of children and parents.

Staff Questionnaire J-2

1	2	3

VALIDATION DECISION

☐ V   ☐ NV

Parent Questionnaire 10

DK	No	Yes

Director's comments on rating _____

For validator _____

_____ _____

_____ _____

_____ _____

_____ _____

_____ _____

J-3. Individual descriptions of children's development are written and compiled as a basis for planning appropriate learning activities, as a means of facilitating optimal development of each child, and as records for use in communications with parents.

1	2	3

Staff Questionnaire J-3

1	2	3

Check documents

VALIDATION DECISION

☐ V   ☐ NV

Director's comments on rating _____

For validator _____

_____ _____

_____ _____

_____ _____

_____ _____

_____ _____

Validation/Accreditation Release Form

Please read carefully and sign.

As _____

(Title)

of _____

(Name of program)

which is applying for accreditation by the National Academy of Early Childhood Programs, I verify that this program has completed a self-study and Program Description, which is attached, and request a validation visit to verify the Program Description. I certify that I understand the accreditation procedures, that I knowingly and voluntarily present this program for review. I understand that the Academy may deny accreditation to this program if the Academy determines that this program does not comply with the Academy's Criteria, and that if accreditation is granted it may be revoked upon a determination that this program is no longer in compliance with the Criteria or that this program has failed to comply with Academy procedures. I understand that if accreditation is granted, it is null and void if false information is knowingly submitted to the Academy at any time.

_____

(Name of program)

hereby releases the Academy, the National Association for the Education of Young Children, and their employees and agents from liability in connection with actions and decisions taken with respect to this application for review and accreditation, except for cases of gross negligence or willful misconduct.

I further understand that this program has the right of advance notice of the validator(s) who will conduct the on-site visit and date(s) for the visit. I understand that I may request a different validator if a conflict of interest exists with the person assigned. I enclose the validation fee in the amount of $

Please make check payable to NAEYC.

_____

Signature of program director or authorized administrator

_____

Name (Please print)

_____

Date

Section 8

Preparation for the Validation Visit

Validation Process Verification Form

Preparation for the Validation Visit

What is the purpose of the validation visit?

After the self-study is completed, if you decide to seek accreditation for your program, the next step is the validation visit. Objective observers, called *validators,* visit your center to verify the Program Description. The purpose of the validation visit is to verify that the Program Description is an accurate description of the program's daily operations.

Before validators are assigned, Academy staff examine the Program Description to determine that it is complete. Academy staff may conduct phone interviews to obtain additional information for incomplete or unclear areas of the Program Description. Academy staff may advise the center to record additional information or to delay seeking accreditation until program improvements have been made.

What does *validate* mean?

The validators do *not* make the accreditation decision. The accreditation decision is made by a three-person Commission of early childhood experts who consider the validated Program Description and use their professional judgment to determine if the overall quality of the program merits accreditation. The validator's role is to verify the accuracy of the Program Description that will be received by the Commission. The validation process is similar to an agreement process. For example, if the program reports that it does or does not meet a criterion and the validator agrees, then the item is validated (whether or not the criterion is met). Similarly, if the program reports that it does or does not meet a criterion and the validator disagrees, then the item is not validated. For example, the program might report that it does not have adequate materials because that is an area it would like to improve. However, the validator finds evidence that the program does have adequate materials. In this case, the criterion is not validated because the validator disagrees, but she reports the reason for the item being not validated and writes the director's comments about the item on the form.

Who are the validators?

Validators are early childhood professionals who live within driving distance (within 100 miles) of the program. Validators are selected by the Academy. They meet the Academy's qualifications which include having a college degree in Early Childhood Education or Child Development or equivalent, experience working with young children and administering programs for young children, and personal characteristics including good observation and communication skills and high standards of professional and ethical conduct. Validators are trained for their role by the Academy. Validators are paid expenses only.

Validators are assigned by the Academy. Validators are required to report any conflicts of interest that might make it impossible for them to fairly validate a program. Potential conflicts of interest include situations such as the validator previously was employed or sought employment by the program, had a child enrolled in the program, serves on an advisory board to the program, operates a program in direct competition, and so forth. The names of potential validators are provided to directors at the time the visit is arranged. If they perceive potential conflicts of interest, they may request a different validator.

How many validators come and how long do they stay?

The number of validators and the length of the validation visit depend on the number of children present in the center on a given day.

Enrollment

Level 1	Level 2	Level 3	Level 4
Fewer than 60 children	*61 to 120 children*	*121 to 240 children*	*More than 240 children*
One validator— one day	Two validators— one day	Two validators— two days	Three validators— first day/ two validators— second day

What do validators do?

The validation involves three major tasks:

(1) Validators verify the accuracy of the average rating of the criteria that are observed in classrooms by observing a sample of classrooms and comparing their rating to the center's rating. Validators randomly select classrooms to be observed with an attempt to see all the different age groups. Validators need to observe at least 50% of the groups. Approximately two-thirds of the children enrolled should be present for the visit to be conducted.

(2) Validators verify the accuracy of the administrative criteria by comparing evidence. The validation procedure varies depending upon the evidence that is available for each criterion.

(3) Validators discuss all nonvalidated criteria with the director and record the director's and validator's comments about the Criteria on the Program Description.

How are the observed criteria validated?

To validate Part 2 of the Program Description—Results of Classroom Observations, the validator observes in a sample of the classrooms by using the same Early Childhood Classroom Observation used by the center. In a small center, all classrooms may be observed, but usually the validator will randomly select classrooms to observe, trying to see the different age groups served by the program. Then the validator compares her ratings to the ratings reported by the center (on the Early Childhood Classroom Observation Summary Sheet) for those classrooms she observed.

To make the validation decision, these rules are applied:
- ■ When one or two classrooms are observed, the ratings reported by the center and the validator must agree in order for a criterion to be considered validated.
- ■ When three or more classrooms are observed, there can be no more than one case of a one-point difference and no cases of a two-point difference in order for a criterion to be considered validated.

Below is an example of a validation decision for an observed criterion:

FOR VALIDATOR ONLY													
Ratings of Center & Validator													
GROUPS													
C	V	C	V	C	V	C	V	C	V	C	V	C	V

CRITERION

G-7. **The environment includes many soft elements.**

For example:

Rugs, cushions, rocking chairs, soft furniture, and soft toys.

AVERAGE RATING

VALIDATION DECISION   ☐ **V**   ☐ **NV**

Director's comments on rating _____

For validator _____

In this case the decision would be to validate because out of more than three groups observed there was only one case of a one-point difference. The Program Description form includes space for the director to explain the average rating. In this case, because the rating was below 2.5, the director provided an explanation. If the criterion were not validated, the director and validator would discuss the difference in ratings. The results of the discussion would be reported in the space marked "For validator."

How are the administrative criteria validated?

The validation process for Part 3 of the Program Description—Results of Administrator Report varies depending upon the available evidence for the criterion. The evidence will be the results of Staff and Parent Questionnaires; written documents; interview with the director; or in a few cases, observation of the physical facility.

To be sure that the results of the questionnaires were reported accurately, the validator first examines the original questionnaires. A few items on each are randomly selected, responses are counted and matched with numbers reported by the center. If the summary sheets are not accurate, the director is asked to redo the summary sheets and the Program Description is corrected.

To validate criteria that require written documents, the validator will need to have access to those documents. To help the validator, the director should collect all the required documents in one place or identify their location for the validator on the List of Documents. The List of Documents appears in Section 4 (pp. 75–76) of the *Guide.*

The "validation procedure" column on the Program Description tells the validator what sources of evidence to compare to verify the accuracy of the director's rating of each criterion. If the sources of evidence are consistent, the criterion is validated (**V**). If the sources of evidence are not consistent, the criterion is not validated (**NV**) and the validator asks the director for more information. The possible sources of evidence and the procedures used by the validator are explained below.

Parent Questionnaire number—An item on the Parent Questionnaire relates to the criterion. Validator compares parent responses to other sources of evidence such as director's rating or Staff Questionnaire.

For a rating of 3 to be validated, at least 75% of the parents who returned the questionnaire (or 50% of all the parents, whichever is higher) must answer the question "yes."

Staff Questionnaire number—Criterion appears on the Staff Questionnaire. Validator compares staff responses to other sources of evidence such as director's rating.

For a rating of 3 to be validated, at least 75% of the staff must rate the item a 3 (when there are at least four staff members).

Observe facility—Validator observes the facility to see if criterion is met (for example, **G-22b**—Emergency telephone numbers are posted by telephones).

Interview—Validator interviews the director to verify the information.

Check Staffing Pattern—Validator compares observed staff-child ratios and group sizes with those reported. Validator verifies that chart has been filled out correctly.

Check documents—Validator verifies that the written documents exist and contain the required information.

Sample documents—Validator carefully examines the content of a sample of the multiple documents required (staff records or health forms) using the following rules for sampling.

Rules for sampling—To sample child records, sample from each age group in the program—infants, toddlers, preschoolers, school-agers. Sample from the beginning, middle, and end of each group of documents using a list of enrolled children to verify that forms exist for all of them. Check at least 10 documents; or if there are more than 100 children, sample 10%.

To sample staff records, check 4 selected at random; or if there are 20 or more staff members, sample 25%.

Below is an example of a validation decision for an administrative criterion:

CRITERION	DIRECTOR'S RATING			FOR VALIDATOR ONLY	
				VALIDATION PROCEDURE	
	Not met	Partially met	Fully met	*Staff Questionnaire* E-4	VALIDATION DECISION
E-4. Benefits for full-time staff include at least medical insurance coverage, sick leave, annual leave, and Social Security or some other retirement plan.	1	(2)	3	2 15 0 ¹ ² ³	☑ V ☐ NV
	Director's comments on rating			*For validator*	
	No medical insurance provided.				

In this case the decision would be to validate the director's rating of partially met, because it is consistent with the ratings reported by staff members on the Staff Questionnaire.

What happens when criteria are not validated?

In each case where a criterion is not validated, the validator and director discuss the criterion, and the validator records on the Program Description the results of the discussion.

During the discussion it may become apparent that the center personnel misinterpreted a criterion in assigning a rating. After the validator clarifies the meaning of a criterion, the director may wish to change the first rating. If so, the director makes the change and initials it. Validators may *not* change the director's ratings or their own, but must record the results of the discussion on the Program Description.

How is the validation visit organized?

Charts of the validation tasks and suggested timelines for completing them are provided in this section of the *Guide* (pp. 205–208). These are only samples to aid the validator and director so that all tasks are completed in the limited time available.

At the end of the visit, the director and validator(s) sign the Validation Process Verification Form, verifying that the validator(s) followed the correct procedures during the visit. A copy of the Validation Process Verification Form appears in the *Guide* on pp. 209–211.

What will the director need to do during the validation visit?

The director should plan to be at the center at 8:00 a.m. to meet the validator(s) and should plan to be there until the visit is completed—5:00 or 5:30 p.m. The director should plan to be available to the validator(s) during the entire day, but primarily in the afternoon when the interviews about nonvalidated criteria are conducted. The director will not be needed during the time the validator is observing in classrooms. However, if the director is also a teacher, it will be necessary for her to be relieved of her teaching duties during the afternoon to be available to work with the validator.

What will the staff do?

Be sure that teachers and children are prepared for the validator's visit. Some of the teachers will have their classrooms observed by validators. Teachers should try to behave as naturally and normally as possible. They should also maintain their normal classroom routine. A simple explanation to the children is best, such as, "Today we have a visitor who is watching to see what we do in our school. She will write things down on her paper to help her remember what she sees." The validator may need to interview the teacher briefly after the observation to obtain evidence for the criteria that could not be observed. This interview should take only 10 to 15 minutes. It should take place at the end of the observation period. The director or other available person may need to relieve the teacher for this brief time period.

What special arrangements are needed for validators?

Validators will bring the Program Description that was completed by the director. This same form is used for completing all the validation tasks.
Validators will need
(1) a relatively quiet space with room to work
(2) the original copies of the Parent Questionnaire that were returned to the center
(3) the original copies of the Staff Questionnaire filled out by staff
(4) access to the documents required by the Criteria (see List of Documents, pp. 75–76)

Do not throw away any questionnaires even after they have been summarized on the summary sheets.

Points to remember

(1) The validator does not make the accreditation decision.

(2) The validator's job is to make sure the Program Description is accurate. The discussion of nonvalidated criteria is the director's opportunity to supply any additional information that would be helpful to the Commission.

(3) You and your staff have worked hard in preparation for the validation visit. View it as another step in a series of professional development experiences for you and your center.

Validation Visit Tasks and Sample Timelines
One validator—one day

TIME	VALIDATOR TASK
	Morning
8:00	Validator arrives at center, meets personnel, tours facility, finalizes schedule for completing validation tasks, and observes arrival of children.
9:00	Conducts one or two classroom observations, observing at least one hour in each classroom.
11:00	Interviews classroom teacher(s) for approximately 15 minutes to complete ratings for items unable to observe.
11:30	Begins validation tasks of Program Description—Parts 1 and 3. Verifies reported results of Staff and Parent Questionnaires by sampling a few criteria from each. Verifies reported Staff Qualifications by checking the documentation for a sample of the staff.
	Afternoon
12:00	Lunch break
12:30	Completes validation tasks of Program Description—Parts 1 and 3. Checks documents. Checks Staffing Pattern to make sure it is completed correctly and to verify its accuracy compared to observed staff-child ratios and group sizes. Makes a validation decision for each administrative criterion in Part 3.
1:30	Working session with director to complete validation of Program Description—Parts 1 and 3. Validator and director discuss nonvalidated criteria and validator records director's and validator's comments on Program Description. Writes legibly and in black ink.
2:30	Conducts one classroom observation (if a full-day program; in half-day program, observation time would be earlier and validation of Program Description—Parts 1 and 3 would follow).
3:30	Copies validator's ratings for classrooms observed onto the Program Description—Part 2. Copies center's ratings for classrooms observed from the Classroom Observation Summary Sheet onto the Program Description. Makes a validation decision for each observed criterion on Part 2 of the Program Description.
4:00	Working session with the director and validator to complete validation of Program Description—Part 2. Validator and director discuss nonvalidated criteria and validator records director's and validator's comments on Program Description.
5:30 or 6:00	Director and validator complete Validation Process Verification Form after all other tasks are completed.

Validation Visit Tasks and Sample Timelines
Two validators—one day

TIME	VALIDATOR A	VALIDATOR B
Morning		
8:00	Both validators arrive at center, meet personnel, tour facility, finalize schedule for completing validation tasks, and observe arrival of children.	
9:00	Conducts one or two classroom observations, observing at least one hour in each classroom.	Conducts one or two classroom observations, observing at least one hour in each classroom.
11:00	Interviews classroom teacher(s) for approximately 15 minutes to complete ratings for items unable to observe.	Interviews classroom teacher(s) for approximately 15 minutes to complete ratings for items unable to observe.
11:30	Lunch break	Lunch break
	When feasible, brief observation of children's lunch time activity is conducted by one or both validators.	
12:15	Completes validation tasks on Center Profile. Verifies reported results of Staff and Parent Questionnaires by sampling a few criteria from each. Verifies reported Staff Qualifications by checking the documentation for a sample of staff. Checks Staffing Pattern to make sure it is completed correctly and to verify its accuracy compared to ratios and group sizes. Assists Validator B in the sampling of documents to validate Program Description—Part 3.	Completes validation tasks on Program Description—Part 3. Checks documents, samples multiple documents such as health records. Compares evidence to make a validation decision for each administrative criterion in Part 3.
1:30	Copies validators' ratings for classrooms observed in the morning on the Program Description—Part 2. Copies center's ratings for classrooms observed in the morning and for the classroom(s) to be observed in the afternoon from the Classroom Observation Summary Sheet onto the Program Description.	
2:30	Conducts classroom observation.	Working session with director to complete the validation of Program Description—Parts 1 and 3. Validator and director discuss nonvalidated criteria and validator records director's and validators' comments.
3:30	Interviews teacher for approximately 15 minutes to complete ratings for items unable to observe. Copies validator's ratings for this classroom onto Program Description—Part 2. Makes a validation decision for each observed criterion.	Break for director and validator if tasks completed.
4:00	Working session with the director and both validators to complete validation of Program Description—Part 2. Validators and director discuss nonvalidated criteria and validator records director's and validators' comments.	
5:30 or 6:00	Director and validators complete Validation Process Verification Form after all other tasks are completed.	

Validation Visit Tasks and Sample Timelines
Two validators—two days

First day

TIME	VALIDATOR A	VALIDATOR B
	Morning	
8:00	Both validators arrive at center, meet personnel, tour facility, finalize schedule for completing validation tasks, and observe arrival of children.	
9:00	Conducts one or two classroom observations, observing at least one hour in each classroom.	Conducts one or two classroom observations, observing at least one hour in each classroom.
11:00	Interviews lead teacher(s) for approximately 15 minutes to complete ratings for items unable to observe.	Interviews lead teacher(s) for approximately 15 minutes to complete ratings for items unable to observe.
11:30	Verifies reported results of Staff and Parent Questionnaires. Assists validator B in sampling tasks required for validating Program Description—Parts 1 and 3.	Completes validation tasks on Program Description—Part 3. Checks documents. Verifies Staff Qualifications and Staffing Pattern.
	Afternoon	
	When feasible, brief observation of lunch time activity is conducted by one or both validators.	
1:00	Lunch break	Lunch break
1:30	Conducts one or two classroom observations.	
2:00		Makes a validation decision for each item on Program Description—Part 3.
2:30		Working session with the director to complete validation of Program Description—Parts 1 and 3. Validator and director discuss nonvalidated criteria and validator records director's and validators' comments.
3:30	Interviews lead teacher(s) observed in the afternoon to complete ratings for items unable to observe.	

Validation Visit Tasks and Sample Timelines Two validators—two days (cont.)

Second day

TIME	VALIDATOR A	VALIDATOR B
	Morning	
9:00	Conducts one or two classroom observations.	Records results of the observations done on the previous day on the Program Description. Records the center's ratings for the classrooms being observed today.
10:00		Conducts one or two classroom observations.
11:00	Interviews classroom teacher(s) for approximately 15 minutes to complete ratings for items unable to observe.	
11:30	Lunch break	
	Afternoon	
12:00	Brief observation of children's lunch activities.	Interviews lead teacher(s) for approximately 15 minutes to complete ratings for items unable to observe.
12:30	Copies ratings from second day observations on Program Description—Part 2. Makes validation decision for each observed criterion.	Lunch break
1:00	Working session with the director and both validators to complete the validation of Program Description—Part 2. Validators and director discuss nonvalidated criteria and validator records director's and validators' comments.	
4:30	Director and validators complete Validation Process Verification Form after all other tasks are completed.	

Validation Visit Tasks and Sample Timelines Two Validators—first day Three Validators—second day

Follow timelines for two validators—two days; except that on second day, Validator C does same activities as Validator A.

National Academy of Early Childhood Programs

Validation Process Verification Form

> **Program Code**

Name of program _____

Date of visit _____

Directions: During the validation visit, the director and validator(s) initial each procedure listed below, verifying that it was properly followed. At the end of the visit, the director and validator(s) sign the form verifying that all procedures were properly followed.

VALIDATION PROCEDURE	PROCEDURE PROPERLY FOLLOWED	
	Director	Validator(s)
Validator(s) meets with director to review validation tasks and plan visit.	_____	_____
Validator(s) briefly tours facility.	_____	_____
Groups are randomly selected to be observed by validator(s) with an attempt made to see as many different age groups as possible.	_____	_____
Validator(s) compares ratings of observed groups to ratings reported by center and makes validation decision for each criterion on Part 2 of Program Description applying decision rules.	_____	_____
Validator(s) verifies accuracy of Parent and Staff Questionnaire summary sheets. (If summary sheet(s) is inaccurate, director redoes summary sheet(s) and corrects Program Description.)	_____	_____

VALIDATION PROCEDURE	PROCEDURE PROPERLY FOLLOWED	
	Director	**Validator(s)**
Validator(s) provided access to written documents required by the Criteria (where information is not available on site, director provides certification by authorized agency or individual of the documents' existence and location).	_____	_____
Validator compares evidence and makes validation decision for each criterion on Part 3 of the Program Description.	_____	_____
Validator and director discuss each nonvalidated criterion, and validator records director's and validator's comments on the Program Description.	_____	_____

For director:

As _____ of _____ ,
       (Title)   (Name of program)
I affirm that all validation procedures described above were properly completed. I affirm that I have had an opportunity to comment about each nonvalidated criterion, that I have read the comments of myself and the validator(s) recorded on the Program Description, and that the comments accurately represent the results of my discussion with the validator(s) about each nonvalidated criterion.

_____
Signature

_____
Date

If one or more of the validation procedures were improperly followed, a written report of the violation must be sent to Academy Headquarters immediately.

For validator:

I _____, as a validator for the National Academy
(Name)
of Early Childhood Programs, affirm that all validation procedures described above were properly completed during this validation visit. I affirm my commitment to maintaining confidentiality regarding all information obtained about this program through the Program Description
and during the validation visit, except as required by law.

_____
Signature

_____
Date

For validator:

I _____, as a validator for the National Academy
(Name)
of Early Childhood Programs, affirm that all validation procedures described above were properly completed during this validation visit. I affirm my commitment to maintaining confidentiality regarding all information obtained about this program through the Program Description
and during the validation visit, except as required by law.

_____
Signature

_____
Date

For validator:

I _____, as a validator for the National Academy
(Name)
of Early Childhood Programs, affirm that all validation procedures described above were properly completed during this validation visit. I affirm my commitment to maintaining confidentiality regarding all information obtained about this program through the Program Description
and during the validation visit, except as required by law.

_____
Signature

_____
Date

Section 9
The Accreditation Decision

The Accreditation Decision

Who makes the accreditation decision?

Accreditation decisions are made by three-person Commissions of early childhood specialists. Commissioners are drawn from a large pool of qualified individuals throughout the country. Each three-person team represents three different states. Using Commissions to make accreditation decisions helps ensure that a national, rather than a local or state, standard is applied. Each three-person team considers between 15 and 20 Program Descriptions in one meeting. Several Commissions meet at the same time, and Commission meetings are held approximately every eight to ten weeks throughout the year.

What information do commissioners receive?

Commissioners consider the validated Program Description. The information on the Program Description includes the director's original report of the center's compliance with the Criteria and an explanation for any criteria that are not met or partially met, the results of the validation, and the director's comments about every nonvalidated criterion. Commissioners do not know the name of the program being considered.

How do commissioners decide whether to accredit a program?

The Commission decision allows for the application of professional judgment within the limits of the Criteria. Commissioners consider the unique aspects of the program, the context in which it operates, and the overall impact of varying degrees of compliance.

For example, a program may have slightly less indoor space than is required, but it may be located in a warm climate where teachers do many activities outdoors. Another example of applying professional judgment relates to staff qualifications. If staff do not meet the required qualifications, the commissioners will look carefully at the training and experience staff do have and also at the curriculum and the quality of interactions among staff and children. A similar situation will occur if group sizes or ratios of children to staff are slightly larger than is required.

The decision to accredit does *not* require 100% compliance with the Criteria. Accreditation requires substantial compliance. Where criteria are not met or partially met, it is important that the director provides the validators and the commissioners with clear information about what the program lacks. Also, when a director feels that a criterion is met through alternate means, it is important to provide an explanation.

Academy staff work with the program director to assist in evaluating and improving the program and in preparing the Program Description. Academy staff are available by phone to answer questions during the self-study. Prior to assigning validators, Academy staff review the Program Description and may communicate with the director to ensure that the Program Description is as accurate and complete as possible.

What options do the commissioners have?

Two decisions are possible: to accredit the program or to defer accreditation until improvements have been made. Sometimes accredited programs receive strong recommendations for improvements that need to be made within a designated period of time.

What happens if accreditation is deferred?

The program receives a detailed Commission Decision Report explaining why accreditation was deferred and what the program must do to achieve accreditation. The program also receives a copy of the Academy's Appeals Procedures that describes the options that exist for the decision to be appealed. Most deferred programs continue to work for accreditation and are eventually accredited.

What happens if the program is accredited?

The program receives a letter of congratulations. The original validated Program Description is returned along with a copy of the Commission Decision Report that provides recommendations for further improvement. Accredited programs receive materials that they can use to promote their accreditation: a certificate, a full-color poster, logo sheets, a sample press release, and multiple copies of a parent brochure describing what accreditation means.

How is accreditation maintained?

Accreditation is valid for three years. During that time, accredited programs are required to submit annual reports. The Academy provides an Annual Report form that is used to indicate any changes that have taken place in the program and any improvements made in response to the Commission's recommendations.

The Annual Report form also indicates the center's compliance with the criteria that are met on an annual basis, such as the annual staff and program evaluation. Failure to submit an annual report may be grounds for withdrawal of accreditation. At the end of the three years, programs complete the reaccreditation process to ensure that high quality is maintained.

Section 10
Bibliography

Bibliography

Specified criteria are reprinted with permission from the following sources:

Auerbach, S. *Choosing Child Care: A Guide for Parents.* New York: Dutton, 1981. (Criterion A-8.)

Community Coordinated Child Care in Dane County. "Dane County Early Childhood Program Standards," Madison, Wis., 1975. (Criteria A-11, B-20, C-4b, C-5, F-3b, G-2, G-9, H-10, H-21, H-22, I-3, I-4, and I-5.)

Comprehensive Community Child Care of Cincinnati. "Child Care Performance Standards." Cincinnati, Ohio. (Criteria A-2, E-10, and I-3.)

Missouri Department of Elementary and Secondary Education. "Standards and Procedures for Voluntary Accreditation of Early Childhood Programs: State of Missouri." Jefferson City, Mo., 1983. (Criteria A-1, A-3, A-5, A-6, B-2, C-1, C-2, E-5, E-7, and J-2.)

Pizzo, P. and Aronson, S. S. "Concept Paper on Health and Safety Issues in Day Care." Mimeo. Washington, D.C.: U.S. Department of Health, Education and Welfare, 1976. (Criteria H-21, I-4, and I-5.)

Texas Department of Human Resources. "Day Care Quality Evaluation/Validation Criteria." Austin, Tex., 1981. (Criteria B-7, D-3, and D-4.)

The following instruments and sets of standards were also used as resources in the development of the Criteria:

Action for Children. "Quality Child Care: What It Is . . . and How To Recognize It." Columbus, Ohio, n.d.

American Academy of Pediatrics. "Standards for Day Care Centers for Infants and Children." Evanston, Ill., 1980.

Aronson, S.; Fiene, R.; and Douglas, E. "Child Development Program Evaluation: Child Care Centers—Center Instrument." Harrisburg, Pa.: Bureau of Child Development Programs of the Pennsylvania Department of Public Welfare, 1978.

Bergstrom, J. M. and Joy, L. *Going to Work? Choosing Care for Infants and Toddlers.* Washington, D.C.: Day Care Council of America, 1981.

California State Department of Education. "Child Development Program Quality Review." Sacramento, Calif., 1982.

Child Care Coordinating and Referral Service. "How to Choose a Good Child Care Center." Ann Arbor, Mich., n.d.

Child Day Care Association of St. Louis. "Standards for Day Care Service." St. Louis, Mo., 1982.

Child Development Associate National Credentialing Program. *CDA Competency Standards and Assessment System.* Washington, D.C., 1983.

Child Development Associate National Credentialing Program. *CDA Competency Standards for Infant/Toddler Caregivers.* Washington, D.C., 1984.

Children's Home Society of Minnesota. "Children's Home Society Day Care Programs Quality Control Checklist."Mimeo. St. Paul, Minn., n.d.

Children's World. "Children's World, Inc., Quality Control Checklist." Evergreen, Colo., 1978.

Child Welfare League of America. "Child Welfare League of America Standards for Day Care Service." New York, 1973.

City of Madison Day Care Unit, Department of Human Resources. "Guidelines for Certification/Recertification." Madison, Wis., 1981.

Community Coordinated Child Care for Central Florida. "Program Audit Assessment Tool." Orlando, Fla., n.d.

Comprehensive Community Child Care. "Selecting Quality Child Care for Parents of Young Children." Cincinnati, Ohio, 1979.

Day Care Evaluation Task Force of the United Way of Greater Rochester. "Day Care Center Evaluation Process." Rochester, N.Y., 1982.

Day Nursery Association of Cleveland Consultation Service. "Preschool Center Evaluation Scale." Cleveland, Ohio, 1963.

Endsley, R. C. and Bradbard, M. R. *Quality Day Care: A Handbook of Choices for Parents and Caregivers.* Englewood Cliffs, N.J.: Prentice-Hall, 1981.

Familiae, Inc. "Standards for Accreditation by Familiae, Inc." Columbus, Ohio, 1981.

Fiene, R.; Douglas, E.; and Kroh, K. "Child Development Program Evaluation: Center Licensing Instrument." Harrisburg, Pa.: Pennsylvania Department of Public Welfare, 1980.

Gold, J. R. and Bergstrom, J. M. *Checking Out Child Care: A Parent Guide.* Washington, D.C.: Day Care and Child Development Council of America, n.d.

Harms, T. and Clifford, R. M. *Early Childhood Environment Rating Scale.* New York: Teachers College Press, 1980.

Hartman, B. "The Hartman Assessment." Mimeo. Santa Ana, Calif., n.d.

KCMC Child Development Corporation. "Agency Assessment/Self-Assessment." Mimeo. Kansas City, Mo., n.d.

Kendrick, R.; Williamson, E.; and Yorck, J. "Finding Quality Child Care." Eugene, Oreg.: Lane County 4-C Council, n.d.

Mattick, I. and Perkins, F. *Guidelines for Observation and Assessment: An Approach to Evaluating the Learning Environment of a Day Care Center.* Mt. Rainier, Md.: Gryphon House, 1980.

Missouri Department of Elementary and Secondary Education. "Choosing the Right Early Education Program for Your Child: A Checklist for Parents." Jefferson City, Mo., n.d.

National Association for the Education of Young Children. "How to Choose a Good Early Childhood Program." Washington, D.C., 1983.

National Association for the Education of Young Children. "How to Plan and Start a Good Early Childhood Program." Washington, D.C., 1984.

New Jersey State Department of Education. "Self-Study Process for Pre-school Programs." Trenton, N.J., 1980.

Oregon Association for the Education of Young Children. "Assessment Criteria Checklist for Criteria for Assessing Early Childhood Programs." Portland, Oreg., 1981.

Oregon Association for the Education of Young Children. "Criteria for Assessing Early Childhood Programs." Portland, Oreg., 1979.

Upgrading Preschool Programs. "The Book of UPP." Mimeo. Phoenix, Ariz., n.d.

U.S. Department of Health and Human Services. *Comparative Licensing Study: Profiles of State Day Care Licensing Requirements, Rev. Ed.* Vols. 1–6. Washington, D.C., 1981.

U.S. Department of Health and Human Services. "Head Start Performance Standards Self-Assessment/Validation Instrument." Washington, D.C., 1981. (DHHS Publication No. 81-31132)

U.S. Department of Health and Human Services. "Head Start Program Performance Standards." Washington, D.C., 1981. (DHHS Publication No. 81-31131)

U.S. Department of Health, Education and Welfare. "Federal Interagency Day Care Requirements." Washington, D.C., 1968. (DHEW Publication No. 78-31-081)

U.S. Department of Health, Education and Welfare. "Guides for Day Care Licensing." Washington, D.C., 1973. (DHEW Publication No. 73-1053)

U.S. Department of Health, Education and Welfare. "HEW Day Care Regulations." *Federal Register* 45, no. 55 (March 19, 1980).

Washington Child Development Council. "Child Development Center Self-Assessment." Washington, D.C., 1980.

The Criteria were developed from a thorough review of the research, and theoretical and practical literature on the effects of various components of an early childhood program on children. The following is a selected bibliography of those sources that were most applicable in developing the Criteria:

Bronfenbrenner, U. *The Ecology of Human Development.* Cambridge, Mass.: Harvard University Press, 1979.

Caldwell, B. M. and Freyer, M. "Day Care and Early Education." In *Handbook of Research on Early Childhood Education,* ed. B. Spodek. New York: Free Press, 1982.

Falender, C. A. and Mehrabian, A. "The Effects of Day Care on Young Children: An Environmental Psychology Approach." *Journal of Psychology* 101, no. 2 (1979): 241–255.

Fiene, R. "Child Development Program Evaluation: Weighing Consensus of Individual Items: What Are the Major Risks to Children in Day Care Centers?" Harrisburg, Pa.: Office of Children and Youth, 1978.

Golden, M. and Rosenbluth, L. *The New York City Infant Day Care Study.* New York: Medical and Health Research Association of New York City, 1978.

Kendall, E. D. "Child Care and Disease: What Is the Link? *Young Children* 38, no. 5 (July 1983): 68–77.

Kilmer, S. "Infant-Toddler Group Day Care: A Review of Research." In *Current Topics in Early Childhood Education,* ed. L. Katz. Vol. 2. Norwood, N.J.: Ablex, 1979.

McCartney, K.; Scarr, S.; Phillips, D.; Grajek, S.; and Schwarz, C. "Environmental Differences among Day Care Centers and Their Effects on Children's Development." In *Day Care: Scientific and Social Policy Issues,* ed. E. F. Zigler and E. W. Gordon. Dover, Mass.: Auburn House, 1982.

Meyers, W. J. "Staffing Characteristics and Child Outcomes." Washington, D.C.: U.S. Department of Health, Education and Welfare, 1977. (ERIC Document Reproduction Service No. 156 341)

Phyfe-Perkins, E. "Children's Behavior in Preschool Settings—A Review of Research Concerning the Influence of the Physical Environment." In *Current Topics in Early Childhood Education,* ed. L. Katz. Vol. 3. Norwood, N.J.: Ablex, 1980.

Phyfe-Perkins, E. *Effects of Teacher Behavior on Preschool Children: A Review of Research.* Washington, D.C.: National Institute of Education, 1981. (ERIC Document Reproduction Service No. 211 176)

Prescott, E. "Relations Between Physical Setting and Adult/Child Behavior in Day Care." In *Advances in Early Education and Day Care,* ed. S. Kilmer. Vol. 2. Greenwich, Conn.: JAI Press, 1981.

Prescott, E.; Jones, E.; and Kritchevsky, S. *Day Care as a Child-Rearing Environment.* Washington, D.C.: National Association for the Education of Young Children, 1972.

Ruopp, R.; Travers, J.; Glantz, F.; and Coelen, C. *Children at the Center: Final Report of the National Day Care Study.* Vol. 1. Cambridge, Mass.: Abt Associates, 1979.

Smith, P. K. and Connolly, K. J. *The Ecology of Preschool Behaviour.* Cambridge, England: Cambridge University Press, 1980.

U.S. Department of Health, Education and Welfare. *Appropriateness of the Federal Interagency Day Care Requirements.* Washington, D.C., 1978.

Index

Note: The Criteria for High Quality Early Childhood Programs are indexed in *Accreditation Criteria and Procedures of the National Academy of Early Childhood Programs.*

A

Academy 10–11, 223. *See* National Academy of Early Childhood Programs
  definition of xi
Accreditation 10, 13, 116, 195, 204
  decision ix, 3, 215
  length of 216
  maintenance of 195, 216
  meaning of ix–x
  process 3
  withdrawal 195, 216
Accreditation Criteria and Procedures of the National Academy of Early Childhood Programs xi, 3, 19, 47
Accreditation system 3
  goals of ix
  purpose of 3
Administration 4, 53–56, 157
  criteria 53–56, 86–88, 170–176
Administrator 115–116
  definition of xi
Administrator Report 3, 9, 11, 12, 43–77, 116, 118, 120, 157, 201
  directions for use 45–46
  instructions 47
  purpose of 45
  results of 116, 118
  sample copy of 47–65
Annual report 216

C

Center Profile 10, 12, 45–46, 115, 117, 120, 121–129
  sample copy of 66–74, 121–129
Centers
  definition of xi
Change 9–10
Child Care Information Service 10
Children 17

Classroom Observation Summary
Sheet 13, 18, 41–42, 115, 118, 119, 130, 200
  sample copy of 41–42
Collaboration ix
Commission ix, 3, 117, 121, 199, 204, 215–216
Commissioners 10, 115, 117, 120, 215–216
  definition of xi
Conflict of interest 195, 200
Criteria ix, 3, 4. *See* Criteria for High Quality Early Childhood Programs
  not applicable 116, 119
  not met or partially met 118–119, 130, 157, 215
Criteria for High Quality Early Childhood Programs 3, 17, 19, 45, 47, 83, 103, 195
  components of xi, 4
  compliance with 3, 10, 116, 117, 130, 157, 195, 215, 216
  development of xi
Curriculum 4, 130
  criteria 26–33, 48, 84, 136–145, 158–160

D

Definitions xi–xii, 21–22
Director 115–116, 120
  as evaluator 45–47, 75
  as observer 17, 19–20
  definition of xi
  role in self-study 11–13
Documents 47, 201, 202, 204
  List of 75–76, 201, 204

E

Early Childhood
  definition of xi

Early Childhood Classroom
Observation 3, 9, 11, 12, 13, 15–42, 118
  definition of xii
  directions for 17–18
  length of 17
  ratings 17–20
  reporting results 116, 118
  sample copy of 19–40
  sample Summary Sheet 41–42
Evaluation 4, 157
  criteria 64–65, 91–92, 192–194
  of program 9, 10
Evidence
  sources of 17, 20, 47, 83
Examples 19, 20

G

Green book. *See Accreditation Criteria and Procedures of the National Academy of Early Childhood Programs*
Group xii, 17, 19, 21

H

Health and Safety 4, 157
  criteria 36–39, 58–63, 89–91, 130, 150–155, 180–189

I

Improvement of program 7, 9, 10, 12, 17, 116
Indicators xii, 19, 20
Infants
  activities for 29–32, 140–144
  definition of xii, 21
Interactions among Staff and Children 4, 130
  criteria 23, 25, 131–135
Interview
  director 120, 130, 157, 202
  teacher 17, 20

L

License (licensing)   58, 75, 117, 122, 180

N

NAEYC   10, 195, 226
National Academy of Early Childhood Programs   xi, 10, 11, 226
Nutrition and Food Service   4, 157
   criteria   40, 63–64, 156, 190–191

O

Observation, classroom
   of children   4, 14, 17
   result of   118, 120, 130
On-site visit. *See* Validation

P

Parents   ix, 8, 103–107
   definition of   xii
   in reporting results   104
   in self-study   103
Parent Questionnaire   3, 9, 12, 13, 14, 101–107, 118–119, 120, 157, 201, 202, 203
   directions for use   103–104
   in self-study   103
   results of   116, 118–119
   sample copy of   105–107
   sample Summary Sheet   108
Parent Questionnaire Summary Sheet   13, 104, 108, 118–119, 157, 201
   sample copy of   108
   validation of   157
Parent survey, open-ended   12, 109–112
Physical Environment   4
   criteria   33–36, 58, 130, 146–149
Preschoolers   22
   activities for   29–32, 140–144
   definition of   xii
Professional
   development   204
   judgment   199, 215
   recognition   4
Professionalism   x, 7

Program
   definition of   xii
Program Code   19, 41, 66, 67, 117, 121, 122, 209
   definition of   117
Program Description   xii, 10, 11, 13, 14, 18, 45, 82, 103, 113–195, 199, 215–216
   Center Profile, Part 1   10, 45–46, 66–74, 121–129
   definition of   xii
   directions for
      completing   117–119
   information about   115
   Part 2 of   11, 120, 130–156
   Part 3 of   11, 46, 120, 157–194
   parts of   115–116
   purpose of   115
   review of   215
   sample copy of   120–195
   validation of   130, 157, 197–211
   when to send   116, 119

Q

Quality   17, 19
   of interactions among staff and children   17, 19
   of life for staff   81
Questions
   open-ended   17, 20

R

Ratings   17, 18, 19, 20, 41–42, 46, 47, 83, 116, 118
   average ratings   18, 41–42, 116, 118, 200–201
Release form   119, 195

S

Sampling, rules for   203
School-agers
   activities for   29–32, 140–144
   definition of   xii, 22
Self-evaluation   7

Self-study   ix, 3, 4, 5–13, 116, 195, 216
   benefits of   7, 11
   definition of   7
   how to do   5–13
   length of   8
   parts of   9
   steps of   8–11
   timelines   11–13
   wrong way to do   8
Staff
   definition   xii, 21
   role in self-study   7–12
Staff-child ratios   56, 69–71, 117, 124–126, 177, 215
Staff-Parent Interaction 4, 157
   criteria   49–50, 84–85, 161–165
Staff Qualifications and Development   4, 117, 119, 157, 215
   chart of   46, 72–74, 117, 127–129
   criteria   50–53, 85–86, 166–170
   worksheet for collecting information   77
Staff Questionnaire   3, 9, 12, 13, 14, 79–93, 118–119, 120, 157, 201–202, 204
   directions for use   81–83
   in self-study   81–82
   purpose of   81
   results of   116, 118–119
   sample copy of   84–92
   sample Summary Sheet   93
Staff Questionnaire Summary Sheet   12, 82, 93, 118–119, 157, 201
   sample copy of   93
   validation of   157
Staff survey, open-ended   12, 81–82, 94–99
Staffing   4, 157
   criteria   56–57, 88–89, 177–179
Staffing Pattern   45, 46, 69–71, 117, 124–126, 202

T

Teachers   17, 18, 19, 20
   role during validation   203
Toddlers
   activities for   29–32, 140–144
   definition of   xii, 21
   older   22
   younger   21

Information about the National Academy of Early Childhood Programs

The Academy is . . .

. . . a division of NAEYC that provides
- a national, voluntary accreditation system for high quality early childhood centers and schools
- educational resources and referral for early childhood programs seeking accreditation
- public information about high quality early childhood programs

Information about NAEYC

NAEYC is . . .

. . . a membership supported organization of more than 54,000 people committed to fostering the growth and development of children from birth through age eight. Membership is open to all who share a desire to serve and act on behalf of the needs and rights of young children.

NAEYC provides . . .

. . . educational services and resources to adults who work with and for children, including
- **Young Children,** *the* journal for early childhood educators
- **Books, posters, and brochures** to expand your knowledge and commitment to young children, with topics including infants, curriculum, research, discipline, teacher education, and parent involvement
- Informed advocacy efforts at all levels of government and in the media through the **Public Affairs** division of NAEYC
- An **Annual Conference** that brings people from all over the world to share their expertise and advocate on behalf of children and families
- The **Information Service,** a centralized source of information sharing, distribution, and collaboration
- **Week of the Young Child** celebrations sponsored by NAEYC Affiliate Groups across the country to call public attention to the needs and rights of children and families
- **Insurance plans** for individuals and programs

For free information about the Academy, and membership, publications, or other NAEYC services . . .

. . . call NAEYC at 202-232-8777 or 800-424-2460 or write to NAEYC, 1834 Connecticut Avenue, N.W., Washington, DC 20009-5786.